T0329205

CAMBRIDGE CLASSICAL STUDIES

General Editors

F. M. CORNFORD, D. S. ROBERTSON, F. E. ADCOCK

II

MODE IN
ANCIENT GREEK MUSIC

MODE IN ANCIENT
GREEK MUSIC

by
R. P. WINNINGTON-INGRAM

Reader in Classics in the University of London;
formerly Fellow of Trinity College,
Cambridge

CAMBRIDGE

AT THE UNIVERSITY PRESS

1936

CAMBRIDGE
UNIVERSITY PRESS

University Printing House, Cambridge CB2 8BS, United Kingdom

Cambridge University Press is part of the University of Cambridge.

It furthers the University's mission by disseminating knowledge in the pursuit of
education, learning and research at the highest international levels of excellence.

www.cambridge.org
Information on this title: www.cambridge.org/9781107480261

© Cambridge University Press 1936

First published 1936
First paperback edition 2014

A catalogue record for this publication is available from the British Library

ISBN 978-1-107-48026-1 Paperback

CONTENTS

PREFACE

THOUGH the title of this monograph may recall Monro's *Modes of Ancient Greek Music*, it was not chosen with conscious reference thereto, but because only so could its scope be described. In fact, the two books have a similar aim: to discover the nature of the Greek modes rather than the origins or development of the scale-system. If my work will stand comparison with his in scholarliness and lucidity, I shall be well content. Monro found himself able to come to a definite conclusion, namely that mode in the true sense was absent or unimportant in Greek music. There was therefore no occasion for him to proceed to the further question: what particular modalities are there exemplified? But his conclusion has seemed to most scholars unacceptable; and there are divergent theories about the modal values of the notes in the various Greek scales. Though agreeing that Greek music was at one time certainly, probably always, modal, I cannot find that the evidence justifies us in deducing anything like a symmetrical scheme of tonalities: there are hints and suggestions, but from these we cannot proceed to dogmatism. Yet, if the conclusions of this monograph are few and indefinite, I feel that it may nevertheless be useful if it has presented the issues and the evidence clearly. I have foregone, so far as was possible, the aid of analogy and of *a priori* assumptions. In all probability Greek music was closely related to that of the contemporary Orient, and recent writers do well to stress this fact. But, before we can profitably use our knowledge of this background, we must first know what precise features of Greek music we can set against it; and nothing can tell us this except the literary evidence, supplemented by the surviving melodies. Here, then, the evidence of musical documents is examined, such as it is; but it is the literary evidence that bulks largest. It may be objected that this procedure is in the nature of things unlikely to elucidate a musical art. This may well be so. But the literary evidence provides us with data for which any satisfactory system of hypotheses must account; and a critical re-examination of it seemed to be desirable. I can at least hope that something has been achieved in matters of detail, even if no sweeping generalisations are offered.

The book is addressed primarily to students of Greek music and is of a somewhat technical nature. However, in order that it may be intelligible to other students of musical history, I have tried to limit the amount of Greek embodied in the text; and it will be found that in most cases such passages are either translated or paraphrased. Two Greek words I have used freely: ἁρμονία (harmonia) for a mode of the classical period, τόνος (tonos) for a key (or whatever it may be).

My thanks are due to the Council of Trinity College and to the Managers of the Craven Fund, who have generously assisted my researches at different times: to the former I owe a special debt, which I hope to have a further opportunity of acknowledging. Mr A. H. Fox Strangways has kindly helped me with advice and information. I have had the benefit, not for the first time, of Professor J. F. Mountford's criticisms at more than one stage in the writing of this work; and he has very kindly read it in proof. Though he is in no way responsible for the views expressed in it, the fact that it has been submitted to his judgment makes me less diffident in offering it to that of others. For I doubt if anyone has ever completed a book upon Greek music without feeling acute dissatisfaction both with his subject and with himself.

R. P. W.-I.

BIRKBECK COLLEGE
LONDON: *January, 1936*

NOTE. The following editions have been used for references: for Aristoxenus, Meibom (1652); for Aristides Quintilianus, Jahn (1882); for Ptolemy, Düring (1930); for Cleonides, Nicomachus, Gaudentius and Bacchius, von Jan (1895); for Plutarch, Weil and Reinach (1900), though in some cases references to the pages of Wechel were more convenient.

CHAPTER ONE

§1. INTRODUCTION

INSPIRATION to the study of Greek music comes to most of those who have felt it from wonder at the musical legislation of Plato and Aristotle, from references to music in the Greek poets, from a realisation of the way in which music permeated Greek life from the Homeric period onward. The student soon finds, however, that his researches lead him into dusty places. The modes, the ἁρμονίαι that seemed so powerful for good or evil to the philosophers, must be sought among the controversies of professors, in dry manuals, out of date perhaps centuries before they were written, or in actual melodies that may in some cases be no more than the hackwork of their own late day. By delving in such places we can learn something. We can learn about the forms and structure of scales, as they are presented in Greek theory. But a scale is a mere list of notes. If we are to begin to have a conception of the kind of music written in it, we must know something of the relationships of the notes that it contains, the hierarchy of their importance. For the democracy of atonality seems to be a discovery of the modern world. The smallest set of notes that the savage sings tends to group itself round a tonal centre. More highly developed music has more complicated relationships; and in some musical cultures these have been worked out in considerable detail. It is the aim of this essay to set out what can be discovered about this aspect of the Greek modes, about the internal relationships of their notes.

It is not a simple task. Probably only actual melodies in adequate numbers, in complete preservation, and of unequivocal interpretation could give us the information we are seeking. Such a collection is not available; and the common measure of agreement between modern authorities upon this matter of modes is not great. It cannot be settled with finality in the present state of the evidence; but it may be useful to re-examine that evidence as a whole and see what conclusions, if any, can be based upon it. First, the few remarks of ancient writers that seem to have a direct bearing on the subject are examined. Then such of the evidence as bears upon particular modes is collected. Thirdly, the more general question of mode and key is discussed for the purpose of discovering to what extent mode may have been submerged by key in the course of development of Greek music.

The task is not made easier by the subtle nature of mode. Mode is essentially a question of the internal relationships of notes within a scale, especially of the predominance of one of them over the others as a tonic, its predominance being established in any or all of a number of ways: e.g. frequent recurrence, its appearance in a prominent position as the first note or the last, the delaying of its expected occurrence by some kind of embellishment. The modern major scale is an instance of a mode. But there is little occasion to use the term, unless variety of mode is present: and in the classical music of modern times the only alternative to the major mode is the minor, the distinctness of whose character from that of the major has been much impaired by the development of harmony, since the use of minor chords in the developed major key blurs the aesthetic distinction between them. Harmony is indeed a factor antagonistic to mode, and mode an obstacle to the progress of harmony. But harmony played a small part, if any, in Greek music; and our evidence shows fairly conclusively that variety of mode was present there during the classical period, and was present centuries later, when the bulk of our extant fragments was composed and when Ptolemy wrote his *Harmonics*. But it would be a mistake to suppose that mode meant precisely the same thing at all epochs.

There is one word in Greek that is particularly associated with modal variety; it is ἦθος, which is best translated "character" (or transliterated "ethos"). It occurs alike in

Plato and in Ptolemy; but it can hardly have had exactly the same significance for all who used it. This ascription of inherent character to modes is not confined to Greece; but it is conspicuous there because of the fame of certain writers and the moral interpretation they put upon modal character. It would be out of place here to discuss the reasons that led them to this doctrine. It is more relevant to express some scepticism whether musical elements can in themselves possess such clearly marked characters at all. Many other factors enter in. Mode may be defined as the epitome of stylised song, of song stylised in a particular district or people or occupation; and it draws its character partly from associations contracted in its native home, reinforced perhaps by the sanctions of mythology. This is true of the Chinese *tyao*, the Indian *rāg*, and the Arabian *maqam*; and probably of the Greek ἁρμονία. The colour of each mode, each type of song, is precisely felt; and there is great reluctance to combine them by modulation. But, as the commerce of music breaks down this reluctance, the associations gradually fall away; and, though there may still be modal variety of a sort (scales differing in the internal relationships of their notes), the characters of modes must now depend principally upon purely musical differences: they will be less trenchant, and the affinities of mode and subject-matter will be less clearly marked. Again, even within the strictly musical sphere the structure of scales becomes more clearly defined, both in practice and in theory, and, in consequence, systematised.

With these preliminary remarks we can embark upon our task.

§2. THE DIRECT EVIDENCE OF ANCIENT THEORY

Modern musical theory gives to every note of the scale a designation (tonic, mediant, sub-dominant, etc.) which indicates its place in the scheme of relations that underlies our harmonic system. The Greek theorists used a nomenclature which goes back ultimately to the position of strings on the lyre[1]. In itself it implies nothing about the functions of the notes; nor is there any term in Greek theory that corresponds to e.g. the modern "tonic" or suggests a hierarchy of importance among the notes of the scale. Nor do the Greeks anywhere treat the question specifically. It is perhaps permissible to conclude from this that modality in their music was a vague and elusive element, which they were unable to reduce to system; and indeed mode is an elusive thing.

All that we find is a number of passages dealing with the note Mese, which may or may not have a bearing on this question. They may be considered in two groups.

(a) Aristotle (*Met.* 4, 1018 b 29) remarks that Paranete is prior to Nete in point of order (κατὰ τάξιν), Mese being the ἀρχή or starting-point. Clearly he is contemplating the arrangement of notes in the scale rather than their functions; but he regards Mese as the natural standard of reference. We now pass to Aristotelian Problems xix, 33, a text upon which far-reaching conclusions have been based. Why, it is asked, is a descending scale more harmonious (εὐαρμοστότερον) than an ascending one? As so often, more than one answer is suggested. "Is it that in this order we begin with the beginning (ἀρχή)—since Mese, the leader (ἡγεμών), is the highest note of the tetrachord—but in the reverse order with the end (τελευτή)? Or that low notes after high ones are nobler and more euphonious?" The second explanation appeals to a supposed aesthetic fact; the first takes a specific example of downward movement and interprets it in terms of the theoretical structure of the scale. For in Problem 47 we find the same use of ἀρχή and τελευτή for the notes that bound the tetrachord. Clearly then τελευτή here means the end or lowest note of the tetrachord Meson, not necessarily of a complete melody; and this passage by itself provides no evidence that melodies ended on Hypate or began on Mese or that either note had any particular modal function. The most

---

[1] See Diagram on p. 85.

that we can say is that, unless such a melodic sequence had in fact been common, it would probably not have been used as an instance; and that, if there are other grounds for believing that in some types of music there were cadences upon Hypate, then it is very likely that the writer was thinking of such cadences.[1]

(b) The passages just considered deal primarily with the order of notes in the scale. In the Problem, however, Mese is called "leader"; and the expression occurs also in Plutarch.[2] It suggests predominance of some kind, and leads us to a number of passages which clearly contemplate not the order, but the functions of notes. Cleonides (202, 3 Jan) says: ἀπὸ δὲ τῆς μέσης καὶ τῶν λοιπῶν φθόγγων αἱ δυνάμεις γνωρίζονται, τὸ γὰρ πῶς ἔχειν ἕκαστον αὐτῶν πρὸς τὴν μέσην φανερῶς γίνεται: that is, the other notes have a functional relationship to Mese. But this tells us nothing directly about musical practice. Aristotelian Problems xix, 20 and 36 are more important. Both ask in effect the same question. Why is it that when Mese is out of tune the whole melody is disorganised and all the other strings sound out of tune, whereas when one of them is out of tune itself alone is affected? Their answers are different. That of 36 recalls Cleonides: the other notes are

[1] Cf. Monro, *The Modes of Ancient Greek Music*, pp. 45 ff. This passage is often quoted as evidence that Greek melody had a general tendency to fall. In itself it will not bear such an interpretation. Primitive melody has, it is true, such a tendency; and in considering the origins of scales we can postulate it (cf. p. 26). But the Greek music in which we are interested is not primitive; and the evidence for its having this character is precarious. The vocal notation with its downward alphabetic series and certain passages where scales are read downwards are not conclusive proof of a melodic tendency. We read scales upwards: is this evidence of a preference for ascending movement? A sounder basis for this view is perhaps the doctrine of the genera, if we are to explain the lower varieties by the attraction of the lowest note of the tetrachord. But, unfortunately, both the origin and employment of the enharmonic and chromatic genera are by no means clear.

[2] *De musica*, § 112 (Weil et Reinach). Ruelle emended the text of the Problem by inserting καὶ before ὀξυτάτη, thus turning ἡγεμών into a predicate and so relating it to the tetrachord Meson; we could then compare the usage of Ptolemy, e.g. 54, 6: ὁ ἡγούμενος τοῦ τετραχόρδου (φθόγγος), of Nete Synemmenon. But Plutarch uses ἡγεμών as a simple synonym for Mese, without reference to the tetrachord. Forster (*The Works of Aristotle*, Vol. VII, Oxford translation) is thus right to retain the MSS. reading. That ἡγεμών in Plutarch is a noun, in the Problem a feminine adjective, presents no difficulty.

tuned in a certain relationship to Mese, and the loss of it means the loss of the "harmonising" element of the scale (τὸ αἴτιον τοῦ ἡρμόσθαι). That Mese was the string to which the others were tuned is implied by Dio Chrysostom.[1] The answer of 20 is the only passage with a clear reference to actual melody. The cause of the phenomenon is, it is said, that all good melodies (χρηστὰ μέλη, ἀγαθοὶ ποιηταί) constantly recur to this note as they do to no other, and its recurrence acts as a link (σύνδεσμος) binding the notes of the melody together. This apparently simple statement has given rise to much controversy. It has been both affirmed and denied that we have here an attempt to describe the function of a tonic. Among those who affirm it there has not, unfortunately, been agreement what note is meant by Mese. Is it the central note of the Greater Perfect System, Mese "by function" (κατὰ δύναμιν), or the fourth note from the bottom of any species of the octave, Mese "by position", according to Ptolemy's ὀνομασία κατὰ θέσιν?[2] The latter interpretation at least provides modal variety; and some of the fragments seem to support it. But, if we make this the basis of a scheme of tonics, we are in difficulties with the F mode (not to mention yet the non-diatonic genera). Yet this passage does not justify us in picking and choosing, in taking Mese κατὰ θέσιν as tonic in some octaves but not in all. But, in fact, although it is not inherently impossible that this nomenclature

---

[1] Or. 68, 7 (Dindorf II, 234): χρὴ δὲ ὥσπερ ἐν λύρᾳ τὸν μέσον φθόγγον καταστήσαντες ἔπειτα πρὸς τοῦτον ἁρμόζονται τοὺς ἄλλους· εἰ δὲ μή, οὐδεμίαν οὐδέποτε ἁρμονίαν ἀποδείξουσιν· οὕτως.... It should be observed that even those passages which speak of Mese as a kind of *Stimmton* hardly have a bearing on the query of the Problem, unless it retained some kind of modal predominance in the actual melody. To-day instruments are tuned to an A, but that note need have no modal predominance.

[2] V. infra, p. 64. This was the early view of Westphal, in which he was followed by Gevaert in his *Histoire*. The latter sings a palinode in *Les Problèmes musicaux d'Aristote* (pp. 194–200). But Stumpf (*Die pseudo-Arist. Probl. über Musik*) prefers his earlier view. C. Sachs seems to adopt it in his discussion of the Seikilos-Skolion (*Musik des Altertums*, p. 63). Mountford (*New Chapters in Greek Literature*, Second Series, p. 167) holds that "the fragments seem to indicate that in all the diatonic modes, and in the Mixolydian chromatic, the fourth note ascending was the tonal centre", but makes no dogmatic statement. Cf. p. 70, n. 1.

is earlier than Ptolemy, it seems that the Problems never envisage any musical unit larger than the central octave of the Greater Perfect System or use any other nomenclature than the dynamic. Further, the explanation of Problem 36 (together with the passages of Dio and Cleonides, which are clearly related to it) must refer to Mese κατὰ δύναμιν, and it would be rather surprising if Problem 20 did not also.

But, granted the writer is referring to this Mese, is it certain that he is attempting to describe it as a kind of tonic? Gevaert put forward a different interpretation, which has been developed by Emmanuel.[1] Mese κατὰ δύναμιν is indeed a note of frequent occurrence in extant pieces. But frequent occurrence is not an infallible indication of the tonic, which may not in fact be heard till the very end of a melody. Gevaert finds the reason for the stated phenomenon in the fact that Mese alone forms part of the usual range of all the modal scales and thus acts as a link or bond between them. Emmanuel refines the conception: "la mèse, en effet, n'est pas seulement l'ombilic du système général par la place centrale qu'elle y occupe. Elle est un centre d'émission sonore, une sorte de foyer d'où émane comme un rayonnement, en permanence". To which it may be replied that frequency of repetition is certainly *one* of the many ways in which a tonic may be established, and one which it would be easy to notice; that, while Gevaert's explanation is no explanation at all of the frequent use of Mese *within a single mode*, Emmanuel's ingenious concept is difficult in itself and hard to reconcile with his own theory of the modes, which embraces tonics and finals and, in effect, dominants and mediants, to which, naturally, Mese is differently related in the different octaves. This peculiar property of Mese complicates matters still further. Was it then so clearly marked as to draw an attention to itself which was never paid to the tonics and finals?

[1] Gevaert, *l.c.*; Emmanuel, article on Greek music in Lavignac's *Encyclopédie de la musique*, vol. i, p. 452.

It seems then that the Problem states that Mese (κατὰ δύναμιν) is, not simply (as in Problem 36 and in Dio) the *Stimmton*, but also—what is quite another matter—the tonic (or something like a tonic) of all good melodies. What are we to make of this? There would appear to be only three interpretations possible.

(i) We can accept the statement at its face value and hold that this was the only kind of tonic the Greek musical art ever knew. This was the view of Monro, for whom the difference between "modes" was merely one of pitch. It is however open to fatal objections, notably that it cannot adequately account for the differences of character (ἦθος) so commonly ascribed to them. Macran's theory that each octave-species has Mese (κατὰ δύναμιν) as tonic and takes its character from Mese's position in it, high or low, is hard to disprove, but has little to support it except this one passage of the Problems. The fragments give no countenance to it.[1]

(ii) The Dorian octave is the kernel of the Greater Perfect System. Mese, the central note of the latter, is the highest note of one of the standard tetrachords of the former and was almost certainly the tonic of Dorian melodies. This octave was predominant in theory; and, though we cannot assert that the Dorian mode was equally predominant in practice, it had very great prestige. Thus, it is possible that here the writer is confining either his vision or his praise to the Dorian. The former hypothesis is perhaps not very likely in view of the general terms of the text. But may it not be that, when it is implied that a melody which did not employ Mese in this way could not be a good one, we have before us the work of a disciple, less broad-minded than his master, who had read the praise unreservedly given by Aristotle (for educational purposes) to the Dorian alone and had elevated it into a

---

[1] Monro, *op. cit.* Macran, *The Harmonics of Aristoxenus*, Oxford, 1902. For criticisms of Monro see the review by H. Stuart Jones in *ClRev.* 1894, and J. F. Mountford's article in *JHS.* XL (1920), pp. 18–20.

general principle of tonality?[1] There is still a third possibility.

(iii) We may accept it as true, but true only for a limited period, that which saw the systematisation of Greek musical theory by Aristoxenus. When we come to examine the bearing of that system upon our enquiry, we shall see what reason there may be to infer from it a standardisation of tonality in practical music. First, however, we must abstract from it one portion and consider the seven species of the octave (εἴδη τοῦ διὰ πασῶν).[2] For upon them the most popular theories of the Greek modes have been built.

---

[1] *Pol.* viii, 1340 *b* 4, 1342 *a, b.* However much of genuine Aristotle there may be in the Problems, they contain demonstrable modifications of his views. In particular, Butcher points out (*Aristotle's Theory of Poetry*, p. 133, n. 1) that Problems xix, 27 and 29 state the doctrine of *Pol.* viii, 1340 *a* 28 in an exaggerated form.

[2] See Diagram on p. 85.

CHAPTER TWO

§1. THE EVIDENCE OF THE SPECIES
OF THE OCTAVE

THE modes are indeed often simply equated with the species. It is attractive. We find them enumerated by Aristoxenian writers in association with the modal names, Dorian, Phrygian, Mixolydian, and the rest. Even the term ἁρμονία was sometimes applied to them.[1] They can be compared with the modal system of the Roman church, where similar variety of character is ascribed to similar scales. It may well be near the truth. Yet it is rash to accept a simple identification of them with the ἁρμονίαι in practical use in, for instance, the fifth century. The species are known to us only as part of the systems of Aristoxenus and Ptolemy. There is evidence for earlier forms, and it seems probable that the species are systematised surrogates of less uniform scales and display a greater symmetry than did their forerunners. It is rasher still to found upon this symmetry a theory of tonics such as those we find in the works of Westphal and even later writers. It is rashest of all to base such a theory upon the species of the fourth and fifth, into which Aristoxenus may have analysed those of the octave. It has often been put forward that the fundamental differences between the Dorian, Phrygian, and Lydian modalities are connected with the three different positions the semitone can occupy in a tetrachord.[2] This may be true. But, if we are to believe it, it must be on the evidence, not of Greek theory, but of the fragments and of analogy. We shall see later what light the former have to

---

[1] This is a legitimate inference from Aristoxenus, *Harmonics*, p. 36, 30 (Meibom), where Westphal's emendation is to be accepted. Compare also Aristides Quintilianus 11, 6 ff. (Jahn) and my comments on p. 56.

[2] E.g. by Riemann, *Handbuch der Musikgeschichte*[3], 1, p. 171, who has been followed by subsequent German writers (see below, pp. 16–21). Compare also Laloy, *Aristoxène de Tarente*, p. 90. Note that, the octave having been analysed into a fourth and a fifth, the essence of the fifth has still to be determined. Is it to be analysed into another and similar tetrachord plus a disjunctive tone (Riemann), or completed with a mediant so as to produce a major or minor triad (Emmanuel)?

throw. Analogies are certainly to be found. For instance, if the conclusions of Z. Idelsohn's researches are well founded, the religious music of ancient Palestine employed the three types of diatonic tetrachord, and by the mode of employment showed that they were felt to have different emotional characters.[1] This is interesting and carries such weight as an analogy can. The reasons for doubting that Greek theory gives much countenance to the view that tetrachordal types are modally significant are as follows:

(a) Though the species of the octave had been enumerated before Aristoxenus, there is no evidence for any theorising about fourths and fifths. Indeed, Eratocles, who receives from Aristoxenus (6, 21) modified praise for his work on the octave, is reproached for failing to make a preliminary demonstration of the species of the minor consonances and of the laws of their melodious collocation. To call attention to the lack of observation of the earlier theorists of something that is *ex hypothesi* so fundamental is only a variety of the argument from silence. But it tells slightly against the hypothesis.

(b) The works of Aristoxenus are unfortunately fragmentary. To judge simply by the surviving portions of the *Harmonics* his concern with the minor consonances seems to be to give a theoretical basis to the consecution of intervals in any system rather than to analyse the species of the octave into components important in themselves; and consecution (τὸ ἑξῆς) is the subject in pp. 59–60, where he contemplates the combination of tetrachords of *any* species by conjunction and disjunction. It is always a matter of difficulty to decide how far later writers have reproduced the Aristoxenian doctrine uncontaminated. The only authority who directly relates the species of the octave to those of the fifth and fourth is Gaudentius (346 f. Jan), and there is a feature in his list which undermines our confidence in it as a *significant* analysis.[2]

---

[1] Cf. Sachs, *op. cit.* p. 31.
[2] His division of the Dorian makes its focal point (on this hypothesis), not Mese, but Paramese. Reinach (*La musique grecque*, p. 42 n.) deserves quotation: "la division indiquée par Gaudence n'est pas inspirée par la considération de la

Gaudentius is probably a fairly late writer, but there is earlier evidence for this kind of thing. Thrasyllus (ap. Theon. Smyrn., p. 48 Hiller) defines ἁρμονία (as instances of which he gives Lydian, Phrygian, Dorian) as συστημάτων σύνταξις. Tetrachord, pentachord, and octachord have just been given as instances of systems. The categories overlap; a ἁρμονία is itself an octachord system. The point of Thrasyllus's definition must be that the octave is composed of a fourth and a fifth. And, as the species of the octaves vary, so must those of the minor consonances that compose them.[1] If Aristoxenus divided the seven modal octaves into particular species of the fourth and fifth, then he was not followed by the authors of most of the Aristoxenian handbooks. If he did not, in any case his system was bound to lead sooner or later to analyses of this sort. It by no means follows that they give us the clue to the tonality of the modes.

(c) No writer ever uses the modal names in speaking of the species of the fourth. Thus the use of the terms "Lydian (Phrygian, Dorian) tetrachord" which is so common in modern works on the subject gives a misleading impression. The lack of interest in any species but the first (the so-called Dorian) is almost complete. Nor is there a suggestion anywhere that the *origination* of scales by tetrachord-building made use of any other.[2]

(d) This theory is partly suggested by the symmetry of the species in the orderly system of Aristoxenus, and especially by the nomenclature of the "Hypo-" species, of which it

tonique; elle me paraît être une recette purement mécanique pour construire les sept octaves."

[1] Cf. Aristides Quintilianus 57, 32 J: ἐκ δὲ τούτων (sc. συστημάτων) αἱ ἁρμονίαι. And by ἁρμονίαι he presumably means octave scales, as in 11, 6 ff. Compare also the conception of the octave as the first συμφωνία ἐκ συμφωνιῶν (Nicomachus 252, 12 Jan; cf. Ptolemy 50, 14 Düring).

[2] Riemann, indeed, notes the avoidance of the terms in the Greek writers (Riemann-Einstein, *Musiklexikon*[11], p. 654); nor does he suggest that the non-Dorian scales *originated* in the combination of non-Dorian tetrachords, but rather that they were found to consist of them. Abert admits the greater importance of the "Dorian" ("das vornehmste Tetrachord, das Dorische": Adler's *Handbuch der Musikgeschichte*, p. 32). It is a pity that we do not know precisely when these names became obsolete for the species of the *octave* (see p. 52).

appears to give an intelligible explanation by assuming that e.g. the Hypophrygian consists of the same species of the fourth and fifth as the Phrygian combined in the reverse order. But it is by no means certain that the Hypo- octaves had in each case a close relationship to the mode from which they have borrowed the latter half of their names, still less certain that they had in each case the same. A brief discussion of a difficult subject must suffice here. The terms are earlier than Aristoxenus, who speaks of Hypodorian and Hypophrygian *keys* (τόνοι) in the theory of his contemporaries or predecessors. The lists he gives (37, 18 ff.) present difficulties, for which I offer no solution. It should at any rate be remarked that the Hypodorian name occurs in a position where we should not have expected it. Heraclides Ponticus (ap. Athenaeum 624 *e*) refers to the Hypodorian ἁρμονία, and it is noteworthy that Athenaeus (or his authority) was not certain of the significance of the first element in the compound. Nor were those who named the Hypermixolydian (*v. infra*). For, if Hypo- had implied a recognised relationship, Hyper- would hardly have been used to name a scale which merely exceeded the Mixolydian at the opposite end of the series to the Hypo- octaves and bore no structural relation to it. Yet there must have been some motive for the adoption of these names in the place of older ones. The symmetry would prove an attraction in itself to the systematisers; and, if in one case (or even two) there was an affinity between the pairs, this might have carried the others (or other). Between Lydian and Hypo- lydian such an affinity is highly likely. The Hypolydian is (if not certainly, at least on the balance of probability) the surrogate of the "slack" Lydian of Plato, the ἐπανειμένη Λυδιστί of Plutarch. The term Hypolydian may have come into use as a convenient means of distinguishing the two Lydians without the need for epithets.[1] The Hypodorian was a later

---

[1] Plato, *Rep.* 398 *e*; Plutarch, *de mus.* § 157 (where in view of the preceding sentence it is reasonable to take ἐναντία τῇ Μιξολυδιστί of the order of intervals). I should be inclined to suggest that the Hypolydian was the first of the new names, were it not that it is the only one that is not vouched for apart

version of the Aeolian; and, though the characters ascribed
to the latter and to the Dorian in Athenaeus vary considerably, both were of Hellenic origin and *may* have had analogous
scale-construction (*v. infra*, p. 26). But, if the plausible
hypothesis that sees in the Hypophrygian a survival of an
Ionian mode be true, it is not easy to believe that it was merely
an inverted form of Phrygian: not only is one name Greek,
the other barbarian (this might not signify much in view of
the remarks of Athenaeus at 624 *d*), but they were apparently
classified by Aristotle as "practical" and "enthusiastic"
respectively.[1] This transitional stage in the nomenclature of
the Greek scales is shrouded in mystery; but transition there
was, and the symmetry of the later arrangement may be in
part delusive.

(*e*) In another and most important aspect the very symmetry of the Aristoxenian scheme appears to make nonsense
of such a theory. I refer to the doctrine of the genera. In the
system of Aristoxenus the chromatic and the enharmonic are
on the same footing exactly as the diatonic. Indeed, in the
propositions of his third book, unless other genera are named,
it is always the enharmonic with its ditone and pyknon that
is envisaged; and he tells us expressly that earlier theorists
concerned themselves with the enharmonic alone (2, 7). Yet
a theory of tonality that is based on the species of the minor
consonances is in difficulties over any genus but the diatonic.
The difficulties are as follows: in the Phrygian and Lydian
scales the shapes of the tetrachords waver, the supposed tonics
(meeting-places of fourth and fifth) shift their position with
the mutations of the genera, and to such a degree that it is

from the lists of species of the octave: it is not in the early lists of τόνοι, nor is it
mentioned in the *Problems* like the other two. This might be mere chance; but it
might even mean that the name originated with Aristoxenus. We come back to
the questions: when were the species named (as such), when did they lose their
names?

[1] Though caution is necessary in inferring marked differences in scale-
structure from differences of recorded ethos, it is noteworthy that the classification of Aristotle (*Pol.* 1341 *b* 32) thus cuts across the nomenclature of the
species. There is no justification for regarding the Aeolian-Hypodorian and
Ionian-Hypophrygian as "slack" forms of Dorian and Phrygian respectively.

hard to suppose the melodic flavour remained the same. Thus, for instance, the lower tetrachord of the chromatic Phrygian is (in the natural key) C♯ E F F♯; the "tonic" G has disappeared, and instead of a semitone between two tones we find two semitones at the upper end above a large incomposite interval. Still more remote is the enharmonic, bounded by C and F; one would imagine that such a tetrachord must have had a "Lydian" rather than a "Phrygian" flavour.[1] Again, the enharmonic tetrachord of the Lydian is bounded by the middle notes of the pyknon (μεσόπυκνα), which are unlikely to have received modal emphasis. The chromatic Lydian, of the form C C♯ E F, is interesting; for this type of tetrachord not only occurs in Byzantine music and modern Greek folk-song, but is apparently to be found among our fragments (v. infra, p. 40 and n. 1). It is therefore noteworthy that it is then employed in a manner anomalous by Aristoxenian standards and unallowed for by the notation of the keys. This is a serious crux, but scholars have not faced it frankly. They tend to enumerate the species of the fourth in diatonic form only, and to illustrate the genera from the standard (or "Dorian") tetrachord only; and so they gloss over this very serious difficulty. For there is no reason to suppose that variations of genus were more characteristic of music in the Dorian than in other modes.[2] Laloy is an honourable exception. In an interesting passage[3] he maintains that this giving of the same name to scales so dissimilar must date from an epoch "où les différents modes tendaient à se fondre les

---

[1] It may be observed that the enharmonic Phrygian of Aristides (v. p. 26), though the G is missing, preserves the same extremes as the normal diatonic form.

[2] There is only a remark attributed to Aristoxenus by Clement of Alexandria (Strom. VI, 279): προσήκει δὲ εὖ μάλιστα τὸ ἐναρμόνιον γένος τῇ Δωριστὶ ἁρμονίᾳ, καὶ τῇ Φρυγιστὶ τὸ διάτονον. M. Emmanuel shows discretion in disposing of the genera before he embarks upon "les modes barbares" at all. But such a method would only be justifiable on the assumption of the text. He rightly observes that these modes had been well hellenised before they assumed the forms in which he gives them. Had they then not also been endowed with the chromatic and enharmonic varieties that he gives for the Dorian group?

[3] Op. cit. pp. 243 ff.; cf. RPh. XXIII (1899), pp. 239 ff.

uns dans les autres, où l'abus des modulations avait engendré une sorte de syncrétisme, où la musique grecque prenait le goût des gammes omnimodales, c'est-à-dire, au fond, uni-modales....Quant aux modes véritables...chacun avait non seulement son ordre qui lui était propre, mais aussi ses intervalles préférés, sa tessiture favorite et ses anomalies spéciales." It is indeed rash to assume that every ἁρμονία known to Pindar and the tragedians possessed diatonic, chromatic and enharmonic forms. Now, we may hold that the theoretical system was factitious and misrepresented the musical facts; we may hold, with Laloy, that it represented a new music of a less modal type, in which the importance had come to reside with those notes of the scale which did not vary in the mutation of the genera, the "standing-notes", that is, of the Greater Perfect System, whose core was Dorian: at least we must treat arguments based upon its regularities with great caution.

Arguments based on regularities which do not belong to this system, as we find it described by ancient authorities, but have been foisted on to it by modern writers must be treated with greater caution still. I refer to the threefold grouping of modes by Riemann, which has been acclaimed as an important step forward in our understanding of Greek music. I regret that I cannot share this view.

It may have surprised some readers that, in section (d) above, the terminology of the Hypo- modes was discussed with-out more than a passing reference to the prefix Hyper-. Now Riemann (*Handbuch*, pp. 166 ff., § 17 "Die ältesten Skalen") and his followers regard the prefixes as complementary, and, taking as fundamental the Dorian, Phrygian, and Lydian octaves, ascribe to each two "Nebenskalen" with a fixed pitch relationship to it, which is indicated by the prefix; thus the Hyper- scales are a fifth higher, the Hypo- scales a fifth lower than the fundamental octaves. The latter consist of two similar tetrachords (to the type of which they owe their specific character) separated by disjunction; the bye-forms are obtained by adding a similar tetrachord by conjunction, in the one case to the upper, in the other case to the lower tetrachord, and completing the octave with the disjunctive tone at the extreme end (upper or lower) of the scale. So the Dorian group is combined in a compendious scale as from A–b¹ (Hypodorian A–a, Dorian e–e¹, Hyperdorian b–b¹), the Phrygian group as from G–a¹, the Lydian as from F–g¹. By taking the Phrygian and Lydian as retunings of the Dorian octave, the whole group of nine can be brought within the compass A–b¹. The usual equations of Hypodorian-Aeolian and Hypophrygian-Ionian are made; Hyperdorian is Mixolydian, and Hyperphrygian is Locrian (cf. Cleonides 198, 13 J, etc.), the latter being, like the Hypodorian, an A mode, but with different internal structure.

The first comment must be that we know nothing of such a set of *nine* from ancient theory. We find there, on the one hand, the seven species of the octave, combined in a two-octave scale, whose importance is fundamental; we may add an eighth, the Hypermixolydian (*v. infra*), still within the range of the Greater Perfect System; apart from the last no Hyper- names appear, and the Hypo- octaves lie high and not low. There is no hint anywhere that the Greek theorists in constructing compendious scales to embrace a number of modes ever exceeded this limit.[1] On the other hand, we have the system of keys (τόνοι), of which we are told that to the thirteen of Aristoxenus later theorists added two more. The relationship of Aristoxenian keys to the modes is not a simple question, and we shall return to it. Here it need only be noted that there is no mention of nine ἁρμονίαι, nine octave scales, nine keys only. There must be very strong reasons before we can allow that nine modal forms made up the system of "the oldest scales".

Clearly, if the triadic arrangement is fundamental, so must

---

[1] Thus Riemann does not in fact improve matters by compressing his modes within the compass of two octaves *and a tone*.

be the significance of the prefix Hyper-, and it should date from the same stage of systematisation as its companion Hypo-. Yet even supporters of this view have to admit that we hear little of the "Hyperskalen" in ancient writers.[1] It will be well to see just how little and in what contexts we do hear of them; in particular, how often they appear as modal octaves.

(1) The name Hypermixolydian is vouched for by Athenaeus, Ptolemy, and the Aristoxenians. Athenaeus (625 d) speaks of it as a ἁρμονία, Ptolemy (63, 6 Düring) as a τόνος; but the "keys" of Ptolemy are in effect species of the octave, and both Athenaeus and Ptolemy offer the same objection to a Hypermixolydian, that it is otiose. Hypermixolydian is the first of the two names given to the highest key of Aristoxenus's thirteen;[2] and in every other case the first name given is that of an octave-species and is presumably the earlier. Note then (a) that the Hypermixolydian octave remains within the bounds of the Greater Perfect System and forms part, if otiose, of the scheme of octave-species; (b) that the prefix implies no structural relationship to the Mixolydian species,[3] and the key of this name is simply so called, as Ptolemy says, ἀπὸ τοῦ συμβε-βηκότος, ὡς ὑπὲρ τὸν μιξολύδιον εἰλημμένον; (c) that, whether the school of eight keys be early or late, the vaguer use of the prefix is likely to be the earlier; for it could hardly have been

---

[1] E.g. W. Vetter in *RE.*, article on *Musik*, col. 847: "gegen die Hyperskalen bezeigt der Grieche eine gewisse Abneigung". Cf. Riemann, *op. cit.* p. 187.

A criticism of the support claimed for the theory from the mention of σύντονοι and ἀνειμέναι ἁρμονίαι by Aristotle (*Pol.* viii, 7) and of the supposed necessity of providing for differences of pitch may well be relegated to a footnote. Whether these terms had originally a connotation of pitch or how long they retained it cannot be discussed here. It is quite probable that some of the old modes had preferences for a particular tessitura. But on Riemann's own showing (pp. 175–179) it had become possible, by the time of the theorists, to take the various modes at several different pitches, which can only mean that pitch, absolute or relative, was no longer an essential element in them. That Hypo- and Hyper-had this significance in all cases is incredible. Cf. p. 14, n. 1.

[2] Cleonides, 203, 7 ff. J, and Aristides, 14, 13 ff. J, are our authorities for the nomenclature of the Aristoxenian keys.

[3] Riemann's treatment (pp. 193 ff.) of the Hypermixolydian is very unsatisfactory: he seems to overlook the occurrence of the name in the list of Aristoxenian keys. Nor can I understand or reconcile Düring's remarks in *Ptolemaios und Porphyrios über die Musik*, pp. 233, 235.

adopted in a vague sense after it had come to have a precise one; yet it is contemporary with, or even later than, the Hypo- terminology of the species.

(2) It is in Aristoxenian handbooks, in connection with the system of keys, that we find both the Hyper- nomenclature and a triadic grouping. The triads, however, do not emerge from the list of Aristoxenus, whose thirteen keys alone are given by Cleonides, but from the fifteen that are recorded by Alypius and Aristides. The latter says definitely (15, 1 J) that the Hyperaeolian and Hyperlydian were added by later theorists (οἱ νεώτεροι) in order that there might be such a triadic grouping.[1] Thus, it belongs to the latest stage of the system of keys, being made possible by the ultimate additions; there are five, *not three*, triads; and the Hyperlydian is absent from the list of Cleonides. Next for the nomenclature. Alypius uses the triadic names alone. But in Cleonides and Aristides many of the keys have two names, and it is generally (and perhaps rightly) assumed that the first-mentioned are those by which they were known to Aristoxenus; at least that the random use of the epithets Aeolian and Ionian for keys which have no essential connection with the modes of those names is late.[2] Observe then that the whole Hyper- nomenclature is on exactly the same footing as the misuse of Aeolian and Ionian: the Hyperdorian is a second name for the lower Mixolydian (ὃς νῦν ὑπερδώριος: Aristides), the Hyperphrygian (where Hyper- has precise significance) for the Hypermixolydian (where it has not); the Hyperlydian, being a late addition, has no alternative name, and could have none, because with it we have passed beyond the octaves of the Greater Perfect System (it is in fact a repetition at the octave of the Hypophrygian). The natural assumption is,

---

[1] τούτοις ὑπὸ τῶν νεωτέρων προτέθεινται ὅ τε ὑπεραιόλιος καὶ ὁ ὑπερλύδιος, ὅπως γ' ἂν ἕκαστος βαρύτητά τε ἔχῃ καὶ μεσότητα καὶ ὀξύτητα. (This is Jahn's text; we should read προστέθεινται, with the best MSS.) Cf. Ptolemy 58, 2 D.

[2] The fact that Aristides prefixes to the lot: ὀνομάζει δ' αὐτοὺς 'Αριστόξενος οὕτως is countered by such expressions as: ὃς νῦν αἰόλιος, and in any case signifies nothing in an Aristides. Note that the Hyperaeolian, which had no alternative name, *may* occur in the Zenon papyrus (3rd cent. B.C.): see p. 32, p. 40, n. 1.

surely, that the triadic grouping and the application of Hyper-names is a late arrangement of related *keys*; and, unless there are strong independent reasons, we should not draw deductions as to the *modes* from them any more than we do in the case of the Aeolian and Ionian key-groups.[1]

(3) Once only does one of these names occur independently. In the passage already quoted, Athenaeus reprehends those who, with an eye solely to pitch and neglecting the differences of species,[2] posit a Hypermixolydian mode and another beyond (ὑπέρ) that; "for", he continues, "I do not see that even the Hyperphrygian has a character of its own; yet some claim to have discovered yet another new mode, a Hypophrygian." Emendation is unnecessary. The passage in quotation marks repeats and substantiates the preceding criticism. In it the Hypermixolydian appears under its alternative title of Hyperphrygian; the other new mode is, most naturally, the latest addition to the list, the Hyperlydian, which is the Hypophrygian repeated an octave higher. Athenaeus is thus evidence that the Hyperphrygian could be called a "mode" as well as a "key" (in fact his point of view is identical with that of Ptolemy, for whom the two conceptions were indistinguishable). But he is not evidence for an early use of the term, since we cannot assume that he is here following Heraclides Ponticus;[3] still less for attributing

---

[1] On the relation of keys and modes, see Chapter Three.

[2] καταφρονητέον οὖν τῶν τὰς μὲν κατ' εἶδος διαφορὰς οὐ δυναμένων θεωρεῖν, ἐπ-ακολουθούντων δὲ τῇ τῶν φθόγγων ὀξύτητι καὶ βαρύτητι καὶ τιθεμένων ὑπερμιξολύδιον ἁρμονίαν καὶ πάλιν ὑπὲρ ταύτης ἄλλην. οὐχ ὁρῶ γὰρ οὐδὲ τὴν ὑπερφρύγιον ἴδιον ἔχουσαν ἦθος· καίτοι τινές φασιν ἄλλην ἐξευρηκέναι καινὴν ἁρμονίαν ὑποφρύγιον. δεῖ δὲ τὴν ἁρμονίαν εἶδος ἔχειν ἤθους ἢ πάθους, καθάπερ ἡ Λοκριστί. It is possible that εἶδος in the expression τὰς κατ' εἶδος διαφορὰς means, not "species", but "type (of ethos)", in view of the recurrence of the word lower, where the reference is clearly to ἴδιον ἦθος. At the same time the line of argument is so closely similar to that of Ptolemy (cf. 58, 7 ff.; 65, 19 ff.) that it is hard to resist the conclusion that Athenaeus is objecting to these modes, as Ptolemy did, because they did not represent independent species of the octave.

[3] It is sometimes assumed that all Athenaeus tells us here about the modes is taken from the περὶ μουσικῆς of Heraclides Ponticus (cf. 624c). Much of it may be; but actually the direct quotations are limited to a couple of sentences (624c: οὐδ' ἁρμονίαν—Ἴωνας; 624e: αὕτη γὰρ—Αἰολίδα). The excerpts of poetry are presumably from Athenaeus's own collection. Whether the commentary on

to it implications about scale-structure. The exact reverse: he complains that the Hyperphrygian had no independent character (i.e. it simply repeated the Hypodorian ἦθος at a different pitch). But it would have had, if it had had a characteristic tetrachordal structure, and if it was on such a structure that modal character depended. As an illustration of a mode possessing "character or emotion" he quotes the Locrian, which had gone out of fashion after Pindar and Simonides. Clearly it is contrasted with the newfangled ἁρμονίαι he has been discussing. Yet Riemann equates the Hyperphrygian with the Locrian. The latter was an A mode (that we know) or something that could be systematised as an A mode. As to its pristine modality and how it differed from the Aeolian we are as ill-informed as on any of the old modes. The Hyperphrygian of Riemann will not help us. For there is no evidence of any weight to show that his modal groupings were those of the Greek theorists at any period, still less of Greek practice; and we must reluctantly apply to them the same expressive word with which Riemann himself dismissed the triads of Westphal: Hirngespinnst.

§ 2. THE EVIDENCE OF EARLY SCALES

The last section has attempted to establish (a) that it is only the seven species as they stand in the Greater Perfect System that can be regarded as the heirs of the ἁρμονίαι; (b) that it is unsafe to infer too much from the orderly form in which they present themselves to us. It is impossible to neglect them entirely as evidence for the old modes: the modal names were attached to them, and even the term ἁρμονία. But it is equally impossible to take them as they stand as representing the old modes adequately. We must, where possible, go behind them in search of something earlier. Some evidence exists, though

the music and national characteristics of the Hellenic races is from Heraclides is uncertain. But καταφρονητέον οὖν κ.τ.λ. can hardly be, because it is irrelevant to his chauvinistic argument, directed against the Lydian and Phrygian modes rather than against any recent innovations.

it is regrettably slight. It consists of (i) the account in Plutarch of the Spondeion scale and its development in the Spondeiakos or Spondeiazon Tropos, supplemented by accounts of defective scales associated with Terpander and Philolaus;[1] (ii) the scales given by Aristides Quintilianus (13, 7 ff. J) as the modes referred to by Plato in the *Republic*. Where this evidence and that of the species give mutual support, we may be on less insecure ground. The scales in question are set out below:[2]

(i) *Spondeion*: e f(?) a b c̄ǀ
    (later) e ē f a b cǀ (with b̄ dǀ eǀ in the accompaniment)

(ii) *Lydian*: ē f a b b̄ cǀ eǀ ēǀ
    Dorian: d e ē f a b b̄ cǀ eǀ
    Phrygian: d e ē f a b b̄ cǀ dǀ
    Ionian: B B̄ c e g a
    Mixolydian: B B̄ c d e ē f b
    Syntonolydian: B B̄ c e g

---

[1] Plutarch, *de mus.* 1134*f*–1135 *b*, 1137 *b–d*; Arist. *Prob.* xix, 32; Nicomachus 253 J. For an interpretation of this evidence and, in particular, for the relation of the latter scales to the Spondeion see my article in *ClQu.* xxii (1928), pp. 83 ff. There I have shown that there is a solution for the difficulties in these accounts, if we take the genus in question to be enharmonic and not, as is generally assumed, diatonic. The omission of Nete in the Spondeiakos Tropos then leaves a scale with the compass of a minor sixth; and the Trite omitted there *and* in the defective scales is the μεσόπυκνον, just as we are told that the semitone was first divided in the lower tetrachord only. The account of the "accompaniment" in the latter passage of Plutarch is also made much more intelligible. I find that I was partially anticipated by Laloy (*RPh.* xxiii (1899), pp. 132 ff.), who did not however carry the matter to its logical conclusion.

[2] J. F. Mountford compares the scales of Aristides with the species in *JHS.* xl (1920), pp. 27 ff., and defends their antiquity in *ClQu.* xvii (1923), pp. 126–129. Apart from these articles there are two valuable discussions: A. H. Fox Strangways, "The Hindu Scale" (*Sammelb. d. Internat. Musikgesellschaft,* ix (1907–8), pp. 449–511, esp. pp. 474 ff.), and L. Laloy, "Anciennes gammes enharmoniques, II" (*RPh.* xxiv (1900), pp. 31–43). A. Thierfelder, "Altgriechische Musik" (*SIMG.* vii (1905–6), pp. 485–507), is interesting but erratic.

In the list in the text above a line over a note (ē) means that it is raised by a quarter of a tone. It is not certain whether the three-quartertone interval of the Spondeion occurred also in the lower tetrachord and whether it was retained in the Spondeiakos Tropos. Of the scales of Aristides the Lydian is noted in the Hypolydian, the rest in the Lydian key (unless we regard the Ionian and Syntonolydian as in the Hypolydian with Synemmenon). The natural key is used for all for the sake of clearness.

Three points of some importance emerge: (*a*) not all the scales have the compass of an octave;[1] the Spondeion has the range of a minor sixth (plus a quarter-tone originally), the Syntonolydian of Aristides that of a minor sixth, his Ionian that of a minor seventh, his Dorian that of a ninth; (*b*) they are not all complete within their range, the Mixolydian showing an incomposite tritone, the Ionian and Syntonolydian a minor third, while diatonic notes are found alongside enharmonic pykna; (*c*) with the exception of the Dorian they show small sign of having come into being by a process of adding tetrachord to tetrachord (or pentachord) of whatever species, nor can they be analysed on this basis without force.

These are the significant things. Remarks are appended on each of these scales, and a few speculations made. No great validity is claimed for them; for, in the first place, it is not certain that the tradition has reached us through Aristides uncontaminated, nor do we know for certain what exact stage of development they represent or how far we can postulate corresponding diatonic and chromatic forms;[2]

---

[1] Plutarch expressly states (§ 177) that Nete was not employed in the melody of the Spondeiakos Tropos, *a fortiori* not in the Spondeion. Cf. the tradition that Terpander added "Dorian Nete" (§ 270). As to the Ionian and Syntonolydian of Aristides many theories have been advanced, and it has been held that his authority was mutilated and the scales originally had the compass of an octave. But it is not agreed at which end this mutilation took place. In view of the traditional heptachord, of the evidence of Plutarch about the Spondeion, of the fact that a feeling for the octave is not an early development of the musical consciousness, it is better to keep an open mind and not exclude the possibility that they are complete as they stand. I would however point out that the limit of the whole set (barring the Lydian) is an eleventh, Proslambanomenos being absent, and that this may have been an early Perfect System. I hope this idea may be more fruitful in another's mind than it has been in mine.

[2] Plutarch (§ 116) seems to imply a stage when the Lydian and Phrygian had an undivided semitone or semitones (τὰ Δώρια, Φρύγια, Λύδια in these passages must refer to early melodies of the "trichordal" type associated traditionally with Olympus: §§ 171, 181, 183). There is somewhat unexpected evidence for chromatic versions in certain planetary scales. That given by Pliny (*Hist. Nat.* II, 19) is in fact the Dorian of Aristides with chromatic intervals, that given by Censorinus (*de die natali*, 13) is the Phrygian. The latter is also to be extracted from the hexameters ascribed by Theo Smyrnaeus (p. 138 Hiller) to Alexander of Aetolia, by ps.-Heraclitus (*Hom. Alleg.* xii) to Alexander of Ephesus. It is a pity if we must decide against the former on grounds of style (cf. J. U. Powell,

secondly, it is a hazardous matter to draw inferences about modality from bare lists of notes. They tell us the kind of thing the old ἁρμονίαι were, but are hardly conclusive for the modality of any particular one.

Spondeion. This type of melody was regarded as Dorian (Plutarch § 108), despite its supposed "invention" by the Asiatic Olympus; and in the development of the Spondeiakos Tropos it was extended to the range of the Dorian octave by the use of Nete (διεζευγμένων) in the accompaniment. Plutarch's account tells us that the inventor passed frequently from both Mese and Paramese direct to Parhypate (and it is thus interesting to find the tritone in those portions of the Delphic Hymns that seem to be reminiscences of this style); but this tells us nothing of a tonic. However, we may probably assume that the tonic was Mese (this again is supported by the Delphic hymns), and that the complete octave was felt as two similar tetrachords combined by disjunction. Indeed, it is likely that a complete diatonic Dorian octave arose independently and influenced the development of the Spondeion.

Lydian. The authenticity of this scale is rightly suspected. The suspicious features are these: (i) alone of the scales it is identical with an octave-species and contains no anomalies; yet the object of Aristides in quoting them was to illustrate anomalous "tetrachordal divisions" (13, 7 J); (ii) it alone is noted in the Hypolydian key, presumably because it was observed to be the Hypolydian species; (iii) it alone is bounded by μεσόπυκνα. It may further be noted that it occurs out of order: with this exception the modes are in Plato's order reversed, last the two mournful modes, then the Ionian, then the permitted modes, Dorian and Phrygian. This suggests

Collectanea Alexandrina, p. 129), as this would have been authority of greater antiquity. In any case this evidence cannot be pressed too far. Scales with nine notes were needed and taken from what source we cannot say. It may be that it was the source of Aristides or a collateral one, and that a notation meant for the enharmonic was interpreted as chromatic in accordance with the music of a later day.

that the companion to the Ionian was lost at some stage and supplied (perhaps at first marginally) by the Hypolydian of the Aristoxenians.[1]

Dorian. This is the normal enharmonic Dorian with the addition of the d below (Lichanos Hypaton), an anomaly by Aristoxenian standards, which was at one time thought to throw suspicion on the scale.[2] The very fact that this note was given a name of its own, Hyperhypate, independent of the tetrachord Hypaton,[3] suggests that it had a specially close relation to the central octave. But for once we are not dependent solely on theory. For this note is used in the second Delphic hymn below a chromatic pyknon; and the manner of its employment there is, in conjunction with Parhypate, to emphasise Hypate. Such a function gives an intelligible motive for the aberration.[4] There is little doubt that Mese served as tonic, and that the analysis of the scale into tetrachords was something more than mere theory. It is not the primary object of this essay to discuss the development of scales, but a few words on the topic are relevant to the question of mode. It is a plausible hypothesis that a primitive tetrachord developed into a heptachord by the addition of one interval of a fourth to another, both fourths being filled up by two approximately equal tones with a

---

[1] There is only one difficulty about this hypothesis. Aristides names the Ionian and Lydian without qualification. This is a misunderstanding of the Platonic text, where (whether we read αἵτινες or αὖ τινες) χαλαραί is rather an epithet than a predicate (cf. Plutarch's ἐπανειμένη Λυδιστί). Now the "slack" Lydian of Plato is probably the ancestor of the Hypolydian species. But it would have needed great perspicacity to supply a Hypolydian in place of a lost "Lydian".

[2] According to Plutarch (§ 183) the tetrachord Hypaton was not employed "in the Dorian melodies". But we have suggested (p. 23, n. 2) that it is only a certain archaic type of music that is in question there: if there is any inference to be drawn, it is that later Dorian melodies did employ it.

[3] Theo Smyrnaeus, p. 88 H (ἡ καὶ διάτονος ὑπάτων); Aristides 6, 30 J, where the extension of the term to the chromatic and enharmonic lichanos is probably incorrect. On the significance of ὑπερ- here see Jan, *Musici Scriptores*, 143.

[4] The fragment from the *Orestes* employs Hyperhypate below an enharmonic pyknon; but its mode is uncertain. See also my article on "Aristoxenus and the intervals of Greek music", *ClQu.* xxvi (1932), pp. 206f.

residual semitone at the bottom.[1] If in the single tetrachord the upper note of the fourth attracted the more attention to itself, within the heptachord Mese, truly so named at the juncture of the tetrachords, was the focus of the melody.[2] Later, the consonance of the octave makes itself felt, and the heptachord becomes an octachord. A downward melodic tendency (such as we can postulate for primitive music) leads to the upper tetrachord being taken from the upper limit, which leaves the disjunctive tone between the two tetrachords. Still Mese is tonic, but the extremes of the tetrachords and the fourths and fifths relating them receive attention. But there is another way of turning the heptachord into an octachord, namely by adding a tone below it to produce an A mode octave. This is the Hypodorian species of the Aristoxenians, which was equated with the *Aeolian* by Heraclides Ponticus. That this was the historical origin and correct musical analysis of the Aeolian can hardly be asserted; but it would be attractive to find an affinity between two modes both indigenous to Greece. The juncture of the tetrachords perhaps remains tonic, while its relation of a fifth to the lowest note is grasped, and the latter obtains modal importance. But this is a hypothesis only and not the only one that could be framed.[3]

Phrygian. This scale, like the diatonic Phrygian octave-species, stretches from d–d[1]. It is thus free from the disadvantage of the enharmonic of Cleonides, namely that the extreme notes of the scale, which may be supposed to have some importance,[4] are transformed. But the g, often assumed to be the Phrygian tonic, is none the less absent. We are, of

---

[1] This would be an instance of the two early methods of scale-construction: by approximately equal tone *distances*, and by larger consonant *intervals*, of which the fourth is the first to be grasped. A downward tendency (leaving the residual semitone at the bottom) is common in simple vocal music. Cf. C. S. Myers, "The Beginnings of Music" (*Essays and Studies presented to William Ridgeway*, p. 574).

[2] Cf. Fox Strangways, *op. cit.* p. 466.

[3] Was the Mixolydian B mode similarly produced by adding a tone at the top of the heptachord? This is less likely. It does not account for the mixture implied in the name or square with the scale of Aristides (*v. infra*). It leaves the disjunctive tone in the air.

[4] Cf. Aristides 57, 29 (quoted on p. 57).

course, largely ignorant of what earlier forms the scale may have had. But Plutarch tells us that in Phrygian melodies of the "Olympic" type Nete Synemmenon occurred (§ 181), and presumably this was one of the modes of the period that encroached on the tetrachord Hypaton (§ 184); further, he implies that there was a stage when one or both of the semitones was undivided (§ 116). Thus, with good-will, we can see in the sequence a b c¹ d¹ a "Phrygian" tetrachord. If the lower part of the scale has already suffered standardisation, we cannot recapture what preceded it. It may be added here that the fragments (notably the Epitaph of Seikilos) show some signs of music written in a *diatonic* D mode with tonic G.

Ionian. There appear to have been two modes of this name, of which one was characterised as "slack".[1] It has been conjectured that the other Ionian mode survived in the systematisation as the Hypophrygian, just as the Aeolian did as the Hypodorian. Whether this be true or not is irrelevant to the scale of Aristides, which represents Plato's mode, the "slack" Ionian, so that there is no means of checking it. The hypothesis of mutilation gives no helpful results: at whichever end it is completed, it is equally unprofitable to see in it either an A or a B mode. There is this further difficulty, that it is uncertain what note is concealed within the minor third. As the scale stands in the Lydian notation, it must be f. Now we do not know whether Aristides found both description and notation in his authority (this is highly probable); but, though he might conceivably have translated the notation into description, he is unlikely to have performed the reverse process. However, it does not follow that whoever it was wrote out the notes knew the essence of the scale.[2] It is equally likely that its true place in the system is from e–d¹ and the "missing" note b rather than b♭. Taking the intervals as they stand, we can only say that in range it corresponds to the traditional heptachord, and its lower half is an enhar-

---

[1] Cf. Plato, *Rep.* 398e; Pratinas, ap. Athen. 624f.
[2] We do not know when the Lydian key attained the pre-eminence.

monic tetrachord of standard type. It is perhaps fanciful to see in the upper half traces of an oriental pentatonic.[1]

Mixolydian. Like the enharmonic octave-species of the name, this scale extends from B to b, but its internal construction differs from it in that the diatonic lichanos, or Hyperhypate, is added to the lower tetrachord, while Mese is lacking in the upper, leaving a tritone at the top of the scale.[2] It is an odd, but not unintelligible, set of notes: the melody would remain for the most part in the close-packed group, the upper b being reached by occasional leaps of an octave (or a fifth). The closeness of the packing has aroused suspicions; and we may remark that nowhere else do we find a pyknon below as well as above Hyperhypate. One or both of the semitones may originally have been undivided. Hyperhypate may have served the same function towards Hypate (μέσων) as was conjectured in the case of the Dorian; or, as Fox Strangways suggests, B B̄ c e, B c d e may have been melodic alternatives. The name implies a mixture, and probably a mixture of Lydian with some Hellenic mode, Dorian or perhaps (since tradition associated it with Sappho) Aeolian. Laloy suggests (*Aristoxène*, p. 97) that it was possible in this mode to give a Lydian flavour to the melody by focussing it about c and f. Fox Strangways (*op. cit.* pp. 484 ff.) provides a most interesting parallel in the Indian Sāman scale: B c d e f, of which the examples fall naturally into two tetrachords B–e, c–f, the former preponderating in some, the latter in others. This is hardly in itself evidence for associating such a tetrachord with the Lydian; but it is suggestive. The question of Lydian modality will be discussed further in connection with the next scale.

Syntonolydian. The scale as we have it is surprisingly brief,

---

[1] For Asiatic influence on the Ionians (and so perhaps on their music) see Athenaeus, 624 d. If such a tendency was common to both Ionian modes, it might help to explain how the other came to be systematised as Hypophrygian.

[2] This may help to explain the achievement of Lamprocles (Plutarch § 156) in recognising where the disjunctive tone lay. What was the view that his displaced? That it lay between the higher pyknon and Hyperhypate? This tone is a kind of counterpart of the disjunctive tone at the fifth.

and various attempts have been made to complete it. It has been made into a G mode by downward extension, while Laloy adds a b c¹ in order to obtain a "Lydian" tetrachord. Neither hypothesis is very convincing; both may contain a germ of truth. For it is improbable that there were three Lydian modes (Syntonolydian, Lydian and "slack" Lydian); and, if the last-named is to be equated with the Hypolydian, it is the Syntonolydian that was systematised as the Lydian octave species (C mode).[1] But a simpler way than Laloy's of establishing a relation between them is to assume that the scale is put in the wrong place in the notation (*v. supra*, *Ionian*), to restore it to the range e–c¹ and suppose that the note concealed by the minor third is b rather than b♭; then, by the addition of the lower c, we get something closely comparable to the octave-species. We need not necessarily suppose that there has been mutilation, but that the scale developed in that direction. To take the existing notes, so small a group has few melodic possibilities. It contains two consonances (by Greek standards): a fourth, e–a; a fifth, f–c¹. The latter must surely have had modal importance, and it is conceivable that, if (and when) the c was added, f was approached by an upward leading-note. It is likely that there was some kind of affinity between the two Lydian modes; and, if the "slack" Lydian was such as to fit into the F octave, this affinity may have had something to do with the fifth f–c¹ and with an upward leading-note.

To sum up, we can only make more or less plausible conjectures about the modality of these scales. In the preceding section it was pointed out how little justification there is from a consideration of the theoretical system of Aristoxenus

---

[1] Plutarch (§ 148) makes this equation, and adds that the Lydian was "high-pitched" (ὀξεῖα). Clearly he, or his authority, takes this as the significance of σύντονος in the compound. There is other evidence for the high pitch of the Lydian (quotations in Athenaeus from Ion and Telestes: iv, 185*a*; xiv, 626*a*); and it may well be true that one of the Lydian modes had such a preference, at least in solo song. But the importance of such associations must have been lost at a fairly early stage. Cf. p. 18, n. 1.

for basing a theory of the modes upon the species of the fourth and fifth. An examination of these unsystematised scales has done something (though nothing so precarious can do much) to modify this judgment. The Phrygian of Aristides *may* display to us a "Phrygian" tetrachord; the Syntono-lydian has a prominent consonance f–c¹; the Mixolydian would explain the Mixolydian name, if the fourth c–f with an upward leading-note were characteristic of Lydian music. But there is still little reason to believe that the Greeks themselves identified their modes by means of the species of the fourth, still less that octave-scales had arisen, as a matter of historical fact, by adding such tetrachords together or adding pentachords to them, in the way that it appears the Dorian octave (and perhaps the Aeolian) arose as a development of that type of tetrachord upon which the analysis of the Aristoxenians is based. The enharmonic form of this tetrachord appears once at least in each of the scales of Aristides (in one case plus an alien note). It can hardly be supposed that this was a primitive feature of all of them. That is to say, there has already been some measure of standardisation. How much further it was carried can be seen from the Aristoxenian handbooks. The scales and their theory were standardised: what happened to the idiosyncrasies of the modes in the practice of music? Only music could tell us; and we must now examine our pitiful store of musical documents to see what light they have to shed upon the question of mode in Greek music.

§ 3. THE EVIDENCE OF THE FRAGMENTS

The following treatment is brief, but, it is hoped, not perfunctory. It is brief, because its object is not to examine every point of interest in these pieces and every hypothesis to which they have given rise, but, partly, to point out where interpretation is certain or probable, partly, to elicit such relationships as there may be between them and Greek musical theory. It may seem strange at first sight that this apparently

important evidence should be examined after that of mere
scales and with such brevity. But there are many things that
detract from its importance. There is the late date of most of
the pieces: though the music about which we are most curious
is that of the classical period, only one of the extant fragments
can be dated with approximate certainty before the third
century B.C. There are many difficulties of interpretation;
and these are not caused only by the mutilations many of the
pieces have suffered. The notes we possess are dead unless we
can reconstruct from them the living melody as it was sung
thousands of years ago. How were they rhythmised? The
presence of a rhythmical notation in some, the poetic metre
in others, provides us with a fairly reliable guide; but, even so,
many details remain uncertain. A more serious question,
perhaps, is whether in actual performance the melody did
not vary considerably, at least in those pieces intended for
solo-singing, from the noted text. Was the melody embellished
to the taste of the individual performer?[1] We may doubt
whether grace played a large part in the early periods, which
were probably marked by a simplicity and a fear of obscuring
the sense of the words. We can be less sure that this restraint
survived till Hellenistic and Graeco-Roman times. Finally,
the musical judgments that have been passed upon these
fragments by modern investigators are so various that some
measure of scepticism is inevitable.[2]

(i) *The Orestes papyrus.* If this is the music that Euripides
wrote, and it well may be,[3] then it is probably the oldest

[1] See Sachs, *Musik des Altertums*, pp. 55, 77, who produces interesting examples
from the music of China and of Corelli.

[2] Full information about the literature of the fragments can be found in
J. F. Mountford's chapter in *New Chapters in Greek Literature*, Second Series,
pp. 146–183, together with the Greek notation of the *Orestes* papyrus, the Aidin
inscription, the Berlin paean and Ajax fragment, and transcriptions into modern
notation of these, the first Berlin instrumental fragment and the Christian hymn.
Reinach (*La musique grecque*) gives transcriptions of all pieces mentioned below
except (ii). Jan's *Supplementum* to *Musici Scriptores Graeci* (Teubner) can still be
consulted for all fragments that came to light before 1899.

[3] Dionysius of Halicarnassus quotes from the score of the *Orestes*, thus proving
it to have been extant till about the date of the papyrus (1st century A.D.?).

piece of Greek music we possess.[1] Brief and mutilated though it is, it presents one feature of interest: it employs alongside an enharmonic pyknon the diatonic Lichanos Hypaton or Hyperhypate. This phenomenon occurs also in the second Delphic hymn and in the scales of Aristides. Indeed, the notes (of the Lydian key) employed are those of both the Dorian and the Phrygian of Aristides, without the two highest.[2] As, however, no single phrase of the melody is complete and the range of extant notes is less than an octave, it is obviously impossible to say in what mode it is written, Dorian, Phrygian, or some other in an anomalous form otherwise unknown to us. Certainly it cannot be asserted, simply because Mese occurs at two of the metrical divisions, that it is the tonic.[3]

(ii) *Tragic (?) fragment in a Zenon papyrus.*[4] The date of the papyrus is probably about 250 B.C., the date of composition unknown. It is very brief, and no conclusions about mode can be reached. The notes employed show a mixture of diatonic with either chromatic or enharmonic (probably the former) and a mixture of keys (it may be Hyperphrygian with Hyperaeolian), resulting perhaps in the use of six notes

---

[1] I am unconvinced of the authenticity of the melody to the opening of Pindar's first Pythian ode, printed by Kircher in his *Musurgia Universalis* (1650). Till recently it was asserted or denied on somewhat inadequate grounds. The question has been reopened by A. Rome (*Les Études Classiques*, I (1932), pp. 3 ff.), who points out suspicious features, hitherto unobserved, and by P. Friedländer (*Die Melodie zu Pindars erstem pythischen Gedicht*, Leipzig, 1934), who defends Kircher. Prof. J. F. Mountford has kindly shown me an article of his which is to appear shortly in *ClPh*. The question is so admirably summed up there that I feel it unnecessary to discuss it here; but see *JHS*. LV (1935), pp. 264 f.

[2] This is to assume that the note E is enharmonic. It might, however, be diatonic, in which case we should have an "undivided semitone" as in the Spondeiazon Tropos. Jan (*Supplementum*) took the genus to be chromatic, but the case for the enharmonic is the stronger. Cf. *ClQu*. xxvi (1932), pp. 206 f.

[3] The interpretation of this piece is complicated (i) by a symbol (which may be an instrumental note) occurring in the line of notation at each close of a dochmius that appears in the fragment, (ii) by what appear to be instrumental notes occurring in the line of the text at two places. If the latter are such, their values are c and f (in the natural key); but they can hardly form the basis for a theory about the mode used.

[4] J. F. Mountford, "A new fragment of Greek Music in Cairo" (*JHS*. LI (1931), pp. 91–100 and Plate V).

separated only by semitones.[1] Such a borrowing from a neighbouring key for the sake of chromaticism would have a parallel in the first Delphic hymn (*q.v.*); it is completely remote from Aristoxenian theory.

(iii) *The Delphic Hymns*. These were inscribed in the latter half of the second century B.C., and the composition of the second hymn is certainly, of the first probably, contemporary. It may be said of both of them that on the whole (though there are anomalies) they illustrate Aristoxenian theory well, partly because they contain modulations of three kinds, of Genus, System, and Key,[2] partly because in large portions of them the tetrachordal structure is clear and the "standing-notes" receive emphasis. Is it because this was characteristic of the music of the period, or because these portions were written in the Dorian (which would certainly be appropriate to religious music) or allied modes? We must consider the two paeans separately and in sections.

(*a*) In the first section (bars 6–33 Jan, ll. 1–8 Reinach-Powell)[3] of the first hymn the λιχανοειδῆ (the second note from the top of each tetrachord) are absent without enharmonic division of the semitone, so that the composer seems to be imitating the archaic style of the old Spondeion.[4] The key is Phrygian. The range is for the most part that of the Dorian octave-species: where this is exceeded by a semitone above and by a major third below, in neither case can it be asserted that there is a change of mode. There is one passing

---

[1] But see also p. 40, n. 1, where various chromatic irregularities are considered together.

[2] Cf. p. 53.

[3] Jan assumed a lacuna of five bars at the beginning of each hymn. The text and notes of the hymns, together with Reinach's transcription into modern notation, can be conveniently found in J. U. Powell's *Collectanea Alexandrina*, pp. 141 ff. and 149 ff. The references are to the lines of the inscription (not, as in Mountford, to those of the music) to facilitate reference, if desired, to Reinach's *La musique grecque*, where these numbers occur above the line of music. It should be noted that in Powell the last nine lines of the transcription of the first hymn are without the necessary key-signature (three flats); in the eleventh bar from the end Θ for O is a justified emendation, but the corresponding note is E♭, not E♮.

[4] On the tritonal effect in this section see p. 24.

use of the tetrachord Synemmenon. Mese appears to be tonic; and the final cadence is from thrice-repeated Mese to thrice-repeated Hypate Meson, while Nete Diezeug-menon derives emphasis from the employment of the note above it.

The next section (bars 34–62, ll. 9–16) uses now the Phrygian, now the Hyperphrygian key: they pass into one another as easily as the Phrygian passes into its tetrachord Synemmenon in the first section; and Synemmenon of the Hyperphrygian is once used here, showing that the music has passed right over to that key. But there is one note (O) which does not belong to either of these keys. It lies a semitone below a chromatic[1] pyknon (in the Hyperphrygian), and thus provides the composer with a succession of three semitones, not allowed by Aristoxenian theory.[2] For an even more extended chromaticism we can compare the Zenon fragment, and there is a chromatic irregularity in one of the pieces in the Berlin papyrus, perhaps also in the Hymn to the Muse. While these are interesting as suggesting that the Aristoxenian analysis was defective, the question arises whether such successions were a feature of the earlier music or a later elaboration. It cannot be answered with certainty, but there is some probability that they date from not earlier than the time when the aulos was able to play a succession of semitones. This it was probably enabled to do by the technical develop-ments of the fifth and fourth centuries, which, though aimed at ease in modulation, may have stimulated new melodic

[1] The genus is certainly chromatic and not enharmonic. This is evidenced by the late date of the composition, by the character of the words set, and by the nature of the anomaly. There is no reason to suppose that a transverse line was uniformly used to distinguish chromatic notes.

[2] On the principle upon which the note O was selected see p. 40, n. 1; it takes the place of the absent lichanos. Emmanuel adopts from Gevaert the term neo-chromatic for a tetrachord $\frac{1}{4}$ $1\frac{1}{4}$ $\frac{1}{2}$ in place of $\frac{1}{2}$ 1 1. But here, in the absence of Hypate Hypaton, if we have to deal with any novel shape of chromatic tetra-chord, it is rather $1\frac{1}{4}$ $\frac{1}{4}$ $\frac{1}{2}$ (overlapping with the regular $\frac{1}{2}$ $\frac{1}{2}$ $1\frac{1}{2}$). I throw out for what it is worth the suggestion that this might have a Lydian flavour, and note that the limits of the melody in this section are Parhypate Hypaton and Trite Diezeugmenon (of the Hyperphrygian): i.e. those of the C mode.

phenomena, never comprehended by theory. This note is used sometimes to produce a succession of semitones, sometimes in connection with the two lower notes of the regular chromatic pyknon so as to give in effect two distinct but overlapping chromatic pykna.[1] This anomaly makes it difficult to discuss the mode and tonality of the passage: Mese and Hypate Meson of the Hyperphrygian receive some emphasis; but the intruding note is not used simply as a leading-note to Hypate, it has importance in its own right and receives the final (and one other) cadence.

The third section (bars 63–end, ll. 16–end) is fragmentary, and the end is lost. It is mainly diatonic and contains reminiscences of the first section, and, like it, is noted in the Phrygian key. In the surviving bars the melody continually emphasises Nete Diezeugmenon. This and other melodic features reappear in the second hymn, where they will be further discussed.

(b) In the second hymn three styles can be distinguished. The first and last sections (bars 6–35, x, 1–14, ll. 1–7, 33–40) resemble the first section of the first hymn in the absence of λιχανοειδῆ, and appear to have the same tonic and final. The melody lies within the strict limits of the old Spondeion (Hypate Meson to Trite Diezeugmenon) with two exceptions: there is a more frequent use of the tetrachord Synemmenon (without Paranete) than in the first hymn, and in the final section we find the diatonic Lichanos Hypaton or Hyperhypate, for which we can compare the *Orestes* fragment and the scales of Aristides. Its function seems to be to emphasise Hypate.[2]

Secondly, there are two passages (bars 66–80, 111–123, ll. 15–17, 23–26) of somewhat similar character to the above, but differing from them in the use of the chromatic in the tetrachord Meson and in the use of the tetrachord Synemmenon almost to the exclusion of Diezeugmenon (though

---

[1] E.g. 45–47 K ∧ M, 47–48 ∧ M O, 51–54 ∧ M O, 55 K ∧ M, 56–57 ∧ M O. Cf. Jan, *Suppl.* p. 11.

[2] Its restoration at the final cadence is certain; its absence from the first section may be accidental.

Paramese occurs); thus, their notes are mainly those of the traditional heptachord, though we have no knowledge of whether a composer ever set himself to compose in the heptachord as such. In the latter section, however, Hyper-hypate appears, and is its final note. Thus, apart from Paramese, we have a Hypodorian octave (a fact that should be noted for what it is worth). Mese and Hypate both stand out clearly, and Paramese, on each occasion of its employ-ment, is reached from Hypate and returns to it by the leap of a fifth. The gaps are too large to admit of certain inter-pretation.

Thirdly, there are three diatonic sections (bars 36–65, 81–110, 124–150?, ll. 8–14, 17–23, 26–30?)[1] in a key a fourth lower, Hypolydian for Lydian. Their principal feature is the emphasis placed upon Nete Diezeugmenon. Two charac-teristic melodic figures are dᴵ eᴵ fᴵ eᴵ and the downward leap of an octave from eᴵ to e (Nete to Hypate): each of these provides two of the four surviving cadences (ἀμπέχει 55, Τριτωνίδος 65, Κεκροπίᾳ 101, φιλένθεον 110; cf. 45, 93).[2] In what modal octave are these sections written, if any? Opi-nions are diverse: Emmanuel holds that it is a type of Dorian, Jan that it is Hypodorian, Reinach and Mountford that it is Mixolydian. If it is Dorian, then it is a different kind from that which we have met previously, being based structurally upon e–b–eᴵ rather than upon e–a–eᴵ.[3] A Hypodorian that pays so little heed to its extreme limits is rather suspicious. More can be said for the Mixolydian: the melody moves mainly

[1] Bars 159–168 are noted in the Lydian, but it is uncertain at what point this key begins. The phrases in this highly fragmentary portion are somewhat reminiscent of the preceding diatonic section; perhaps this modulation at the fourth, without change of mode (or style), served as a transition to the Lydian coda.

[2] The penultimate note of 65 is conjectural.

[3] The validity of the scheme of tonics (or "pseudo-toniques") and finals attributed by Emmanuel to the Greek modes is as hard to disprove as to prove. It is based on the assumption of similarity between Greek and Church modes rather than on the ancient evidence and aims at more precision than that evidence will allow. On one point he may well be right: that Greek music showed a feeling for the major and minor triads that is not revealed in its theory. See p. 46. For the analysis e–b–eᴵ cf. p. 11, n. 2.

within its range,[1] the fourth note from the bottom may have been tonic in this octave-species, as in the Dorian, though we cannot assert it with confidence. However, the upper limit of it is absent (is, indeed, outside the key altogether), so that the fifth so characteristic of other fragments claimed as Mixolydian is impossible of achievement,[2] while to explain the excursions to notes below it as modulations to the Dorian seems rather arbitrary, where there is no apparent change of style or feeling.[3] Further, the joyful character of the words set conflicts with the character elsewhere ascribed to the Mixolydian. This is perhaps not a fatal objection to supposing that the composer is writing in the octave-species of that name, at a time when the whole complex of associations that made the Mixolydian ethos had been broken up. But we may be fairly certain that the old Mixolydian was not a four-square affair of tetrachords such as we find here. For the most striking characteristic of this, as of the other hymn, is the way in which the tetrachordal structure is kept clear and the framework of "standing-notes" in relief.[4] We may, if we will, call it all Dorian of one type or another, or use it to prove the similarity of Mixolydian and Hypodorian to the Dorian. But so easy is it to distinguish the tetrachords, so difficult the modes or octave-species, that it seems as though the composers had set themselves to write in the Changeless System

    [1] Especially within the diminished fifth that forms its lower portion. Support for the Mixolydian hypothesis may perhaps be derived from the scale of Aristides, where we find a group of notes within this compass together with the octave of the lowest note, which may suggest that an octave rise or fall was characteristic of this style. The fact that the octave leaps in the hymn occur between a different pair of notes is not seriously damaging.
    It may be observed that d¹ is an octave higher than Hyperhypate, that these are the only λιχανοειδῆ employed in the hymn in diatonic passages, and that d¹'s relationship to Nete is similar to that which Hyperhypate generally bears to Hypate. I am convinced that there is much still to be learnt from a close study of these hymns.
    [2] See pp. 42 f.
    [3] This applies also to the analysis of such a passage in the first hymn as bars 19–33, where we have, first, emphasis on Nete (19–21), then a reminiscence of the earlier portion (23–24), then Nete again with the phrase f¹ g¹ a♭¹ g¹ = d¹ e¹ f¹ e¹ (27), then a return, through Synemmenon, to the original style.
    [4] We have seen above (p. 16) that this is an almost inevitable consequence of a strict application of the Aristoxenian doctrine of the genera. See also pp. 77 f.

(including, for the Aristoxenians, the tetrachord Synemmenon) primarily, and only secondarily, perhaps, in any particular section of it. Laloy, as so often, has a good word to say (*Aristoxène*, p. 129): "La musique s'habituait peu à peu à n'employer plus qu'une gamme dorienne uniforme, mais chargée d'altérations et de modulations passagères. C'est dans ce style que sont écrits les hymnes delphiques, où il est aussi facile de reconnaître les accidents et les irrégularités que difficile de déterminer le mode dominant. On conçoit que Platon ait combattu cette musique trop libre, où l'impression d'ensemble était détruite par l'abus du détail, et où le philosophe, armé de ses principes, ne savait à quoi se prendre, tant il était difficile d'évaluer le caractère modal, et par suite le coefficient moral d'un art mobile et fuyant."

(iv) *The Aidin Inscription*, or *Epitaph of Seikilos*. The composition and inscription are probably contemporary, and the latter can hardly be earlier than the second century B.C. and may be considerably later.[1] The brief, but intact, melody is diatonic and employs the notes of the Phrygian octave-species (in the Ionian key). In this D mode G is almost certainly the tonic, while the final cadence is from a thrice-repeated G through E to D. There is an interesting feature at the beginning of the piece. The first note is the presumed tonic, which is followed by the leap of a fifth to the higher limit of the piece. Now this is the only place where the melody goes against the pitch-accent of the words.[2] We shall observe a similar phenomenon in the Hymn to the Muse. This melody is the strongest single piece of evidence for the modal use of the species and, in particular, for the attribution of thetic Mese as a tonic to a species other than the Dorian.

(v) *The Berlin papyrus*. The fragments in this collection were written down later than A.D. 156, but may have been com-

---

[1] Mountford, in *JHS*. LI (1931), p. 92, prints an interesting letter on the subject from the discoverer of the inscription, Sir W. M. Ramsay.

[2] On the relation that is observable in most of the extant Greek melodies between the pitch-accent of the words and the rise and fall of the tune see Mountford, *New Chapters*, pp. 164–166.

posed considerably earlier. They are five in number: (*a*) twelve lines of a paean to Apollo in a Hellenistic manner; (*b*) three lines of instrumental notation which may or may not be connected with it; (*c*) four lines of an address to the suicide Ajax, which may be an excerpt from a tragedy;[1] (*d*) three lines of instrumental notation which may or may not be connected with it; (*e*) half a line of a lyric, conceivably connected with (*c*).

(*a*) The melody is diatonic and ranges from Parhypate Hypaton to Paranete Diezeugmenon of the Hyperionian key (transcribed with one sharp, from G to a), a range that includes the Lydian and Phrygian octaves. It is much broken up, as we have it; but we can identify the ends of the musical phrases with some probability as occurring where a single syllable receives notes equivalent to three of Mountford's crotchets.[2] These coincide with the major sense-breaks and never cut badly across the sense (as plausibly restored by Wagner); they divide the piece into eleven phrases of eleven syllables each, rhythmised as follows (regarding only the total values of notes set to each syllable): ♩|♩ ♩♩|♩ ♩♩| ♩ ♩♩|♩. . It is certain that we possess the beginning, possible that we possess the end, of the piece. Of the nine phrase-endings, extant in whole or in part, one closes with d, and three (including the last) with A. It may be that d is tonic, with A also modally important and perhaps final, in which case we have the same (Phrygian) modality as in the Aidin inscription. Four of the cadences, however, have a remarkable rhythmical and melodic feature, ♩ ♪♪ (1), ♩ ♩ ♪♪ (3) being set to the last syllable. Thus a note is

---

[1] The use of the Hyperaeolian key suggests a fairly late date for the melody, as it is one of those added by οἱ νεώτεροι. Subsequent transposition is possible, but unlikely. Cf. p. 19, n. 2.

[2] The rhythmical notation presents a somewhat complicated problem. The most consistent interpretation is to be found in Mountford, *New Chapters*, who follows in the main Wagner's exhaustive study in *Philol*. N.F. 31 (1921). The breaks occur after the words: ⟨κοῦρον⟩, ⟨αὐ⟩λῶν, ⟨κλη⟩δών, Κρ⟨ή⟩τα, κράνας, φωνάν, στέψας, λώβαν, before τῷ Ζεύς, τῷ γᾶς, and at the end of the fragment.

barely touched for the length of a quaver at the extreme end of the phrase; and in three cases this note is G, outside the Phrygian octave; twice it follows the succession B A, once it is reached by a leap from c. This note G also begins the piece. These are highly interesting phenomena, and it is a thousand pities that the melody has not been preserved entire.

(*b*) There has been no agreement as to the mode or species of this fragment, in which the diatonic series of (*a*) is extended as far as Proslambanomenos (E). There is no certainty that we possess a complete phrase; and, though there are similarities between the rhythmical schemes of this and of (*a*), they may be fallacious, and we cannot use them to identify cadences; we cannot, for instance, say that the first line is complete in itself, beginning and ending with A.

(*c*) The five surviving notes do not all belong to the same key. It is best to take O′ K′ I′ A′ as from the Hyperaeolian, with E′ intrusive to provide a chromatic effect not obtainable without going outside the Alypian key-system. We can compare similar phenomena in the first Delphic hymn and the Zenon papyrus. But there a series of semitones was obtained, here a tetrachord of the shape: $\frac{1}{2}$ $1\frac{1}{2}$ $\frac{1}{2}$ in a place where $\frac{1}{2}$ $\frac{1}{2}$ $1\frac{1}{2}$ would be normal.[1] It is interesting to observe that such a chromatic tetrachord was a feature of Byzantine music and can still be heard in Greece, not to look farther afield. The notes can be transcribed as follows: b c′♯ d′ e′♯ f′♯. In the

---

[1] The anomaly in the Delphic hymn can hardly be said to produce a tetrachord of the type $\frac{1}{2}$ $1\frac{1}{2}$ $\frac{1}{2}$, since the lowest note does not occur (but see p. 34, n. 2). But both there and here the intrusive note displaces the normal diatonic lichanos (or paranete). This allows us to see on what principle the sign for it was selected. There Π is displaced by O, which represents the semitone above Π, wherever that is a "standing-note" (i.e. in the Hypoaeolian, Dorian, and Hyperdorian). Here Z′ is displaced by E′; E′ occurs in no key; but, if we look an octave lower, we find that E is the semitone above Z (in the Hypolydian, Lydian, and Hyperionian). O and E′ then represent the raising of a note by a semitone; and E′ should be transcribed as e′♮ rather than f′♮. In the Zenon papyrus, scale-structure is not clear enough to show us on what principle the foreign notes are taken. It looks as though the last three notes (O I K) are a bold modulation (at the semitone, cf. Cleonides 205, 10) from Hyperphrygian to Hyperaeolian and thus correspond to the sequence Π Λ M in the first line. At least so an ancient theorist might have explained what may have been due to an impulse towards chromaticism.

fragmentary state of the piece it is impossible to discuss its mode. It may be noted that e'♯ does not function exclusively as a leading-note to f'♯.

(d) The melody ranges from Parhypate Meson to Nete Diezeugmenon of the Hyperionian key; and so it is improbable that it has any connection with (c). But transcription is so hazardous because of the difficulty of interpreting the rhythmical signs that no conjectures as to mode are worth making. Nor can the handful of notes in (e) be taken into account, except to record that they are taken, if they have been rightly read, from the lower end of the Hyperaeolian key.

(vi) *The Hymn to the Muse.* This is probably not one piece but two, both of uncertain date.[1] It must therefore be considered in two parts. There is one difficulty in transcription: a symbol N occurs, which does not, like the others, belong to the Lydian key.[2] The most plausible hypothesis is that of Reinach,[3] who held that it was imported to represent a note a semitone below Mese. At both instances of its use in the first section it occurs between Paramese and Mese, to which it acts as a leading-note. The compass, Lichanos Hypaton to Trite Diezeugmenon, tells us nothing definite. The piece

[1] Its respect (with one exception noted below) for the pitch-accent argues a date earlier than that of the hymns of Mesomedes, at a time when that accent still exerted its strength. The separation of the two sections was made by Wilamowitz (*Timotheos: Die Perser*, p. 97) and accepted by Reinach (*La musique grecque*, p. 194) and others. There are good grounds for it, apart from the ἄλλως in the MSS., in the subject-matter, the dialect, and the metre.

[2] The reading H of Venetus Marcianus VI, 10 and its descendants can be disregarded. In the diagrams of Aristides also, where other good MSS. have N rightly, this has H; it looks as though the common archetype had N in an ambiguous form. H occurs in the Lydian key, but as chromatic Paranete Synemmenon, equivalent to Paramese (Z) and quite pointless.

[3] *REG.* IX (1896), p. 18. If he is right, the importation is on a different principle from those of the Delphic hymn and the Ajax fragment. For N does not displace M and is actually below it in the series. It only occurs as an ὀξύπυκνον, and its pitch relation to M (always βαρύπυκνον or ἄπυκνον) depends upon whether it is chromatic or enharmonic. The two occur together in the Hypolydian, where N, as chromatic Paranete Diezeugmenon, lies between M (diatonic Paranete Synemmenon) and I (Nete Synemmenon = Mese in the Lydian). This method of borrowing from an allied key is quite intelligible. Note that on this hypothesis the accent of ἀλσέων is respected.

begins and ends on Hypate, as does the first phrase. The opening presents the same phenomenon as that of the Aidin inscription: the melody rises a fifth from the initial note, this constituting the only breach of the pitch-accent laws. There both notes involved were of modal importance; here Hypate certainly is, Paramese (which opens the third phrase) may be. Clearly much depends on the interpretation of N: if the above explanation is correct, Mese (which closes the third phrase) acquires importance and the melody a Dorian flavour.

In the second section I believe the single occurrence of N to be a textual error for M. The compass is extended to Hypate Hypaton; and Hypate (Meson) is the initial and final note and also most prominent in the melody. The Mixolydian octave is exceeded in one occurrence of Trite Diezeugmenon; and Mese seems to have no importance. We find a similar modality in the Hymn to the Sun. In both sections, though the principal notes of the melody are "standing-notes", tetra-chordal structure is not emphasised as in the Delphic hymns.

(vii) *The Hymns of Mesomedes.* The Hymn to Nemesis is ascribable with certainty to this musician of Hadrian's time, and its companion, the Hymn to the Sun, has such similar style that it probably has the same composer.[1] Both pay about the same amount of attention to the word-accent. Both melodies are purely diatonic and noted in the Lydian key. The compass of the latter is from Parhypate Hypaton to Trite Diezeugmenon, but it moves mainly in the fifth from Hypate to Paramese. It begins on Hypate, and a number of the lines (which are complete musical phrases) end on it, including the last and the important break at ἀμέραν (16). If Hypate is the fundamental note, we still need to determine the relative importance of Mese and Paramese. The first phrase, beginning and ending on Hypate, contains leaps from it to Mese and back. For Sachs[2] this fourth is "trei-

---

[1] For a number of other poems probably by the same author, whose music has been lost, see K. Horna, *SBAkad. Wien, Phil.-Hist. Kl.* 207 (1928).
[2] *Op. cit.* p. 60.

bendes Intervall", and even Paramese "steht ein wenig ausserhalb". But for Emmanuel the melody is based upon the fifth, and the employment of Mese in the first line is perhaps "une équivoque voulue". The frequency of Paramese in cadences supports Emmanuel,[1] and we seem to have a modality akin to that of the second and perhaps the first section of the Hymn to the Muse, whether we are to call it Mixolydian or a variety of Dorian. As there, though the principal notes are "standing-notes", there is little emphasis on the tetrachord. Indeed to the modern ear it seems that a feeling for the triad is clearly shown not only here, but also in the Hymn to Nemesis and the Aidin inscription.[2]

The Hymn to Nemesis has in the main the range of the Phrygian octave-species, but descends a note below it on three occasions. Lichanos Meson (c^1 in the key of one ♭) seems clearly to be tonic, and receives ten of the seventeen surviving phrase-endings (those of ll. 6 and 20 being lost, that of 12 uncertain), including major sense-breaks. In addition, Paranete Diezeugmenon (g^1) is the upper limit of the piece and often emphatically treated, while on two occasions the melody falls from c^1 to g at a cadence. That of l. 9 (c^1 a g) recalls the cadence of the Aidin inscription, which this piece closely resembles in modality. Again we notice a feeling for the triad. At l. 13 there is a cadence of some importance on d^1 (Mese), and the melody of the succeeding lines seems to be based on the fifth b♭–f^1 (or the triad b♭ d^1 f^1) till a return is made to the tonic c^1 at the end of l. 15. A final point of interest is that in the opening line (and again at l. 16) a succession of c^1's is preceded by a single d^1 (as if it were an appoggiatura).[3]

[1] *Op. cit.* p. 396. Note in particular the phrase b♭ c^1 d^1 e^1 e^1 (in one flat), which ends three lines.
[2] See p. 36, n. 3.
[3] I collect here a number of phenomena which may or may not have some relation to one another: the opening of this hymn on a note above its apparent tonic, the opening of the Berlin Paean on a note below its apparent final, the cadences in the Berlin Paean which briefly touch this same note, the close of the second section of the first Delphic hymn on the intrusive note, the close of a section of the second Delphic hymn (bar 123, l. 26) on the note below the heptachord.

(viii) *The Christian Hymn*. The papyrus on which this is found is of the third century A.D.; the melody may, of course, be earlier than either the papyrus or the Christian words set to it. The notes employed are all diatonic and extend from Parhypate Meson to Trite Hyperbolaion in the Hypolydian key. Though this is the Hypolydian species, it has not been suggested that the mode is Hypolydian; for the lowest note is quite unimportant and clearly subordinate to Lichanos Meson. The latter acts as melodic final. Is it also tonic? Or is that rôle played by Trite or Paranete Diezeugmenon? We could not be certain without completer phrases and more cadences. For the earlier portions are fragmentary and there is a large lacuna shortly before the end. Nor are the metrical divisions of the hymn easily made out. We cannot thus with any assurance use it as evidence either that the Hypophrygian was based on the fifth from Lichanos to Paranete, or that its tonic was thetic Mese.[1]

(ix) *Exercises in Bellermann's Anonymus*. These are mentioned here for the sake of completeness. In §§ 97–101, 104, of this treatise are included a number of short snatches of melody, noted in the Lydian key, whose object seems to be to illustrate certain rhythmical classifications. As they are so brief, and their origin and date so uncertain, they cannot be taken very seriously. The longest of them has the range of the Lydian octave-species, begins on c and ends on a, shows a feeling for the triad f a c¹, and has been acclaimed, in default of a better, as an instance of the Hypolydian mode (not the Lydian, presumably because it does not conclude on its lowest note).

We may sum up briefly what we have learnt from the fragments. For the most part they are written in series of notes that accord with the theoretical doctrines of Aristoxenus and can be recorded in the Alypian notation. But there are anomalies of two kinds: (i) the Euripidean piece and portions

[1] Note that for Sachs and Emmanuel the Hymn to Nemesis is Hypophrygian and not Phrygian.

of the second Delphic hymn contain a diatonic note in combination with enharmonic or chromatic pykna, and the scales of Aristides suggest that this was characteristic of the old ἁρμονίαι; (ii) there are a number of chromatic abnormalities, occurring in the Zenon papyrus, the first Delphic hymn, the Berlin Ajax fragment, and perhaps the Hymn to the Muse, which we cannot relate to any other information we possess about Greek music, though they may have their analogies elsewhere.

On the question of mode and tonics, the earliest of the tolerably complete pieces, the Delphic Hymns, are for the most part clearly based upon the tetrachordal structure of the Changeless System, including the tetrachord Synemmenon, whose interplay with Diezeugmenon they illustrate; and the principal notes of their melodies are "standing-notes". It is sometimes possible to assert that such and such a note is tonic, but the Dorian is the only mode that emerges with perfect clarity. The later diatonic melodies present phenomena which can be classified as follows:

(a) In the Aidin inscription, the Hymn to Nemesis, and perhaps the Berlin Paean we find melodies based upon the Phrygian octave-species, in which Lichanos Meson (thetic Mese) appears to play the rôle of tonic. If the octave is to be analysed, it must be into a fourth and a fifth rather than into two "Phrygian" tetrachords joined by disjunction.

(b) In the Hymns to the Muse and to the Sun there is a type of melody whose principal note is Hypate Meson; Mese and Paramese have importance, but the basis of the melody is the fifth from Hypate to Paramese, and the range roughly corresponds to the Mixolydian octave-species. In the Delphic hymns we find passages with the emphasis on Nete Diezeugmenon (an octave above Hypate Meson), but the fifth is not there a feature of the melody.

(c) The Christian Hymn seems to be written in the Hypophrygian species; Lichanos Meson is final and perhaps tonic, but beyond this the structure is not clear.

(*d*) The scrap in Anonymus may show us a Lydian analysable into a fourth (c–f) and a fifth (f–c¹).

In most cases these diatonic melodies appear to show a feeling for triads, both major and minor, in contradistinction to the tetrachordal style of the Delphic Hymns. This feeling may be illusory. Even if it is not, we can hardly, in view of the scantiness of the relics, pretend to determine whether such a feeling was present or absent in the diatonic melodies of an earlier period.

These results are rather tantalising, if we wish to discover a systematic scheme of the Greek modalities. Firstly, it may be said that the fragments lend no countenance to the idea that Mese (κατὰ δύναμιν) served as a general tonic in all modes: if that was ever so, it was not at the time most of these melodies were composed. Thetic Mese, on the other hand, appears in some cases to be the tonic of modal octaves, and thus to divide them into a fourth below it and a fifth above. But by no means all octaves are illustrated: in particular, there is no certain case which allows us to say of the F, G, and A modes (the Hypo- octaves) either that the division in these cases was reversed or that thetic Mese was tonic in them also. Thus, though the fragments give some support to the scheme of tonics and modal analysis that has been based on the Aristoxenian doctrine of the species of the consonances, this support is very incomplete and at least as precarious as an earlier section has shown the theoretical basis of it to be. In fact, the final result of our investigation of particular modalities is somewhat exasperating. There are three sources of evidence, the early scales (particularly those of Aristides), the octave-species of Aristoxenian theory,[1] and the fragments; and they fail either to support or to refute one another conclusively.

Lastly, if the modalities of (*a*) and (*b*) are to be called

---

[1] We shall see that they are fundamental to Ptolemy's theory also; and the bearing of his words upon particular modalities will be considered below, pp. 69 f.

Phrygian and Mixolydian, we find them used in setting words hopelessly inappropriate to the character or ethos ascribed to such scales by classical writers. Yet the word ethos had not disappeared from the vocabulary of music: Ptolemy uses it in his attempt to describe the differences between modes and the Aristoxenians in their classification of Melodic Composition. It is probable that these writers in using an old word meant by it something rather less precise than did their predecessors. The various modes with their differing turns of melody still had distinctive characters, even if we are not in a position to seize them. But the complex of factors that had made the old ἁρμονίαι so powerfully moving had been broken up, and even the melodic factor itself to varying degrees standardised. The psychological terms that the Aristoxenians[1] use are perhaps to some extent a legacy from a more full-blooded doctrine of ethos; and it is to be noted that they do not tie ethos down to the modes as such.[2] In this they are truly Aristoxenian; for Aristoxenus himself had a broad and even sceptical conception of ethos.[3] However, this subject, though it had inevitably to be mentioned here, needs a special study to itself.

[1] E.g. Cleonides 206, 10 ff. J.
[2] With the exception of Aristides; see below, pp. 56 ff.
[3] Cf. *Harm.* 31, 16 ff.; Plut. *de mus.* 1142 *f*–1143 *e*.

CHAPTER THREE

§ 1. THE EVIDENCE OF THE ARISTOXENIANS

In the previous chapter we examined evidence bearing upon particular modalities. Though there is uncertainty about details, the fact emerges clearly that during the classical period Greek music possessed a variety of modes and variety was present also at the much later period during which most of the melodies we have were composed, though the modes they illustrate seem of a more uniform type than those at which the old scales allow us to guess. About the intervening centuries we are ill-informed. We have important musical documents in the Delphic hymns; but they are hard to interpret in isolation. On the theoretical side we have the system of Aristoxenus. It is fairly well known to us through his own work and the manuals of Cleonides and others, though there is always the question how far these have transmitted the master's doctrine without modification. So far we have considered only a part of it, that enumeration of the species of the consonances, in particular, of the octave, which it has in common with the system of Ptolemy. But it is a part only, and takes up relatively little space in the manuals. The system as a whole forms a weighty structure, whose centre of gravity is not readily discoverable. Even were this problem solved, it remains to determine how the theory of Aristoxenus was related to the facts of musical practice.

There are two interrelated problems. On the one hand, the system takes cognisance of keys (τόνοι), as well as of species of the octave. We shall have to consider the nature of the former, the relationship of the two concepts and, if they differ widely, the balance of their importance. On the other hand, we receive an impression from other writers that Greek music used (at least at one time) types of melody that varied in emotional character or ethos. The Aristoxenians seem to take little account of ethos. Is this a defect in their theory, or does it represent a change of practice? If a change of practice, does it mean that modal variety had disappeared or merely that the modes had suffered a degree of simplification and their characters become less trenchant? The two problems are immediately related by the fact that the names (derived from Greek and barbarian peoples) with which the characters of the old modes were associated are used by Aristoxenus to describe the τόνοι. Now the development of the τόνοι is one of the obscurer fields of Greek music. That, in origin, they were closely connected with the modes their names and disposition are enough to show. Indeed, some would argue that they are, in essence, the modal species obtained as retunings of the same octave, devoid of all element of absolute pitch; and, to anticipate, it is as such that we find them in the system of Ptolemy. Others hold that the τόνοι of Aristoxenus, in contrast with those of Ptolemy, had the function of modern pitch-keys. We can make no progress till we have elucidated these conceptions a little.

It is a thorny subject, and only a summary treatment of it is possible here. First let it be asserted with confidence that the conception of pitch-keys did arise in the course of Greek theory; then we will justify this assertion by a brief sketch of the history of τόνος.[1]

(1) We start with isolated and unrelated *modes*, some of which may have been associated with a particular tessitura, though more probably their pitch would depend upon the voice of the singer or singers. The various modes could be obtained by retuning one or more strings of the lyre or cithara, when all of them would have roughly the same pitch, or by the use of a separate aulos for each, when the pitch might or might not vary. Technical developments in both instruments made possible scales comprehending more than one mode: thus, the Phrygian might be found below the Dorian on the cithara. Details are completely uncertain in our

[1] Cf. Laloy, *Aristoxène*, pp. 123 ff., 250 ff.; Reinach, *La musique grecque*, pp. 47 ff.

ignorance of the technique and development of ancient instruments. The important fact is that modes could thus be taken at several different pitches. Now the fundamental idea of τόνος is that of a relation in pitch between scales. But by what standard could modal scales be compared?

(2) Gradually there developed, in a kind of fusion, hard to analyse, of theory and practice, a fundamental series of notes, a *system*. Through various stages it reached the double-octave of the Changeless System, in which, theoretically, the modes took their places as species of the octave.

(3) At some point it was realised that the retuning process of (1) involves in effect the transposition of a portion of the system in (2). This solves the problem of relating the modes in pitch; for the system of which they form part (or some particular note of it) acts as a standard. This system itself can be taken at various pitches, and thus we get a number of *keys* named from the octave that they bring into the central range of an average voice. This is the only conception of key that is necessary for the music of the lyre and of choral song.[1]

(4) But from quite an early stage it had been possible to take the same mode at different pitches either by the use of different instruments or of an instrument of extended range (cf. (1)); and this also involves transposition, the removal of an identical series of intervals from one part of the gamut to another. And, whereas in the case of the lyre the gamut of sound involved was quite small, in the music of the developed aulos and in solo-singing by trained voices of different types it was extensive and involved at least three octaves of sound.[2] The τόνοι from this point of view have new functions: to map out the total gamut, to act as a device for getting any melodic group at any desired pitch. In this way the keys lost touch

[1] Add to it the realisation that any consideration of absolute pitch is irrelevant to such τόνοι, and you have the "keys" of Ptolemy (or of the school of eight τόνοι that he mentions: see p. 75).

[2] Considerably more than three octaves according to Aristoxenus (20, 2 ff.); and this is true, when the voices of women or boys are taken into account (ἐκ διαφερουσῶν ἡλικιῶν 21, 8), as they were not by the Greek scheme of notation.

with the modes from which they had derived their names and came to belong rather to different types of voice or instrument.[1]

That this stage was reached and that we are justified in speaking of pitch-keys in Greek theory is clear from the following points:

(a) It is in virtue of such a function that the keys appear in the system of notation. Clearly, so long as the conception of τόνος is limited to that of (3), notation would only be necessary for a limited range, and only Dorian melodies would be noted in the Dorian τόνος, Phrygian in the Phrygian, and so on. But the fragments give us examples of melodies noted in half a dozen different keys (including members of the Ionian and Aeolian groups) and bearing in most cases no relation to the modes of corresponding name.[2]

(b) We shall see that parts of Ptolemy's polemic are unintelligible except as a polemic against pitch-keys.[3]

(c) The existence of two radically different conceptions of key is clear from Aristides, whose dicta on the subject are inconsistent. At 16, 8 J he speaks of three keys, of which the Dorian serves the needs of the lower "activities of the voice", the Lydian of the higher, the Phrygian of the intermediate.[4] This is best explained on the hypothesis of Greif, that these three keys represented three types of voice, three varieties of tenor. It is meaningless of "Ptolemaic" τόνοι, and inconsistent with the statement of Aristides at 15, 12 J that the Dorian is sung (μελῳδεῖται) in its entirety, the other keys only in so far as their range corresponds to that of the Dorian; for in that passage Aristides is describing Ptolemaic "keys" covering the two-octave range of a single voice.[5]

---

[1] Cf. Greif, *REG.* xxiv (1911), p. 253 f.

[2] Bellermann's Anonymus (§ 28) gives lists of keys favoured by different kinds of instruments. The selection of them is intelligible only if we take them to be pitch-keys.

[3] Cf. p. 67.

[4] Cf. Bacchius 303, 3 f. Jan.

[5] If Aristides took the Dorian τόνος to mean a range of absolute pitch, his thought was confused. What is really meant is that only in the Dorian do the limits of the voice and of the Changeless System (the standard of comparison between keys) correspond. Cf. pp. 64 f., 68.

There were thus two very different conceptions to be found in Greek musical theory, for which the sole name of τόνος had to suffice: it is small wonder that there is some confusion of thought. Now in the schemes of notation we find fifteen keys, identical replicas of the Changeless System. This is two more than the number ascribed to Aristoxenus, and the extra keys are represented as additions to his list. Since the keys of the notation are pitch-keys and we hear of them in authors who follow Aristoxenus in many respects, it might seem natural to assume that he also conceived of his τόνοι as pitch-keys. The question is in fact rather more complicated. We shall return to it, when the system of Ptolemy has been examined; for then we shall have all the available facts before us. But for the moment let us consider what is implied by the existence of pitch-keys bearing the old modal names. It involves, unless modal character depended upon pitch alone (which is a discredited theory), a severance of the connection of name with mode and ethos. However, a key, though it may roughly represent the range of a trained voice, or of some instruments, is too large for the range of a single melody, if only to judge by the surviving fragments. A further selection had to be made. Upon what principles was this done, and how did it affect the resulting melody? Was it based upon the seven species of the octave, the representatives of the old modes? If these retained in any way their old vitality, then ethos was not lost, but merely obscured in the theoretical analysis. In that case we should expect that the old names would be used of the species as well as of the τόνοι, and that the former use would have the greater significance. But it is very doubtful if Aristoxenus so used them. They do not occur in this connection in his extant writings, while of the authors of manuals only Gaudentius uses the present tense in naming the species; Cleonides, Bacchius and Aristides seem to imply that this use of the names was obsolete.[1] In Ptolemy, however, we find

---

[1] Cleonides 197, 7 J and Bacchius 308, 19 J: ἐκαλεῖτο ὑπὸ τῶν ἀρχαίων. Aristides 11, 7 ff. J: παρὰ τοῖς παλαιοῖς...ἐκαλεῖτο. Gaudentius 347, 6 J:

the modal names applied to τόνοι which are not pitch-keys but are intimately related to the species (cf. (3) above); and we shall see that there is reason to believe that this use of τόνος belonged also to the centuries preceding him (indeed it must have been the original use). Whether Aristoxenus always or sometimes thought of his τόνοι in this way is a question upon which it is desirable to suspend judgment as yet. Here we will only remark that, if the modal names are applied by a theorist to pitch-keys but not to the species of the octave, then his theory suggests that the old modalities have either disappeared or lost their names.

It will be of assistance in our present quest if we can trace the fate of the doctrine of ethos in the Aristoxenian system. There is one department of it that sheds some light, the discussion of Modulation (μεταβολή). The master's own treatment of it has not survived; his isolated remarks upon it merely relate to the disposition of the τόνοι. But the existence of a more formal treatment in the manuals is perhaps evidence that he did treat it at length. Cleonides (204, 19 J) distinguishes four varieties: modulation of Genus (κατὰ γένος), of System (κατὰ σύστημα), of Key (κατὰ τόνον), of Melodic Composition (κατὰ μελοποιίαν). The first needs no explanation. The second has been taken to refer to modulation from one octave-species to another. But actually Cleonides is precise enough on the point. It is defined as a change from disjunction to conjunction or *vice versa* (which is a change from the Greater to the Lesser Perfect System, and so μεταβολὴ κατὰ σύστημα), a type of modulation which can be illustrated from the Delphic hymns. Ptolemy (II, ch. 6)[1] describes the same phenomenon and shows that it is in effect a modulation of key, the transposition of an identical series to a pitch a fourth higher. But clearly a transitory modulation of this kind, if the melody remains within the same range, will

καλεῖται (but l. 10 ἐκαλεῖτο). It is very unlikely that these writers would ascribe to οἱ ἀρχαῖοι, παλαιοί, in a past tense a terminology used by Aristoxenus.

[1] See pp. 66 f.

in effect produce a modulation of species; and Ptolemy makes clear the difference between it and a simple transposition. It is thus hard to see why this type of modulation should have been distinguished from the third, modulation of τόνος, unless under the latter was envisaged a modulation of key in the modern sense (such a modulation as we find in the second Delphic hymn, from the Lydian to the Hypolydian key or *vice versa*). The last variety is defined as a change of ethos, of which there are three kinds: systaltic, diastaltic, and hesychastic. But ethos is the word associated with the old modes; and, just as Plato and Aristotle give us classifications of them according to ethos, so here Cleonides classifies types of melodic composition in the same respect.[1] But apart from this summary grading (which occurs also in Aristides Quintilianus) Aristoxenian theory tells us no more about ethos.[2] It belongs to the sphere of Melodic Composition; and Melodic Composition is the employment of the elements of Harmonics in actual melody-making and was only included by Aristoxenus as a part itself of Harmonics on second thoughts.[3] Ethos then emerges in actual composition and has no place in the theoretical analysis, so that we are never told by what means, by what process of selection from the raw material of the art, melodies of differing character could be produced. Clearly

[1] On the whole subject see Abert, *Die Lehre vom Ethos*, esp. § 19. This classification has some resemblances to Aristotle's grouping of melodies: for instance, the description of the diastaltic ethos recalls his "practical" type; the systaltic covers part only of the "ethical" type and embraces both the lamentatory and festive modes of Plato. It should be noted that neither this nor Aristotle's classification is of modes simply. It is something more subtle, and recognises that there are a number of elements that produce the total effect.

I retain the term "diastaltic", which is sanctioned by usage. Actually the MSS. of Cleonides, Aristides and Ptolemy reveal that the word was διαστατικός and not διασταλτικός. For Ptolemy see Düring's apparatus at 29, 2 and 106, 14 (where διασταλτικά in A must be a "correction" by Isaac Argyrus). For Cleonides see Jan on 206, 4 and 6. All important MSS. of Aristides have διαστατικήν at 20, 11 J, but διασταλτικός (under the influence of συσταλτικός) at 28, 7.

[2] Cf. Bacchius, 304, 18.

[3] It is not mentioned among the divisions of harmonics in what now goes as Book I (3, 5–8, 10), or by Plutarch in § 364. But it is included in Book II (38, 18), and the manuals, as the seventh and last of its departments. On the motives for this change of attitude see Laloy, *Aristoxène*, p. 167.

this department allows for the possibility that modal distinctions were retained in the music analysed by Aristoxenus; and it is possible also that such retention was a matter, primarily, of selecting an octave-species, secondarily, of treating its various notes according to their old modal values. Now, with one exception, no Aristoxenian ever suggests that ethos was an affair either of the species of the octave or of the τόνοι. The exception is Aristides, to whose evidence we must next turn.

§ 2. THE EVIDENCE OF ARISTIDES QUINTILIANUS

This has been unduly neglected. Aristides[1] is an eclectic, but in strictly musical matters he is generally an Aristoxenian and has been quoted as such above. His evidence is taken separately here, because his treatment of Melodic Composition contains much detail not found in other writers. His source may have been Aristoxenus. If so, some new light is thrown upon the latter's system. If not, here is independent evidence about the practice of Greek music, though not necessarily contemporary Greek music.

The principal interest of Aristides is in education and the educational value of music (to which he devotes the second of his three books); and so in ethos, of which, like Plato and Aristotle, he tends to take a strictly moral view. On it he makes a number of significant remarks.

(a) 8, 12 J. Notes are distinguished in respect of ethos: ἕτερα γὰρ ἤθη τοῖς ὀξυτέροις, ἕτερα τοῖς βαρυτέροις ἐπιτρέχει, καὶ ἕτερα μὲν παρυπατοειδέσιν, ἕτερα δὲ λιχανοειδέσιν. That is to say, the character of a note (in a scale or melody) depends partly on its absolute pitch (for which we can compare 58, 19 ff., 29 ff. on the characteristics of keys), partly on its function in the scale, its position relative to the other notes. This passage, however, dealing with individual notes, does not of itself imply a variety of modes.

[1] His date is uncertain; but he mentions Cicero, and may be as late as the third century A.D.

(*b*) 11, 17. After mentioning the species of the consonances, he gives the old names for these[1] (including ἁρμονία for the octave), and follows this with the modal names of the octave-species. After pointing out that the quality of the octave (ἡ τῆς ἁρμονίας ποιότης) is manifested by the succession of its notes, he concludes the whole section as follows: περὶ μὲν οὖν συστημάτων, ἃ καὶ ἀρχὰς οἱ παλαιοὶ τῶν ἠθῶν ἐκάλουν, ἀρκείτω ταῦτα. This can only be taken with reference to what has preceded. The systems which the ancients called "bases of characters" are the species of the octave, known also as ἁρμονίαι and by the modal names, and owe their quality to the varying successions of intervals which they show *quâ* species of the octave. This is the clearest identification of the old "ethical" modes with the species, upon whatever authority it is based.

(*c*) 19, 10 ff. Chapter 12 of Book 1 contains an analysis of Melodic Composition which goes far beyond anything in the other Aristoxenians. It is there divided into three parts: Selection (λῆψις), Mixture (μίξις) and Employment (χρῆσις). The first merely selects the general range of pitch. "Mixture" is a question of fitting together (ἁρμόζομεν) the various musical elements as analysed in the preceding theory; it is the preliminary strategy, the general lay-out of the composition. "Employment" is the actual melody-making (ἡ ποιὰ τῆς μελῳδίας ἀπεργασία), and is subdivided into conjunct and disjunct movement[2] (ἀγωγή, πλοκή) and, oddly coupled with them, Petteia (πεττεία). This last is defined[3] as follows:

[1] Ἀρμονία for the octave, δι᾽ ὀξειῶν for the fifth, συλλαβή for the fourth are quoted (in Doric form) from Philolaus by Nicomachus (252 J) and Stobaeus (*Ecl.* 1, 21, 7). If this nomenclature is specifically Pythagorean, Aristides is probably confusing the use of ἁρμονία for the harmonic framework, e a b e¹ (cf. Aristotle ap. Plut. *de mus.* §§ 226 ff.), with its use for a modal octave. But is there any real reason to suppose that it is Pythagorean? Δι᾽ ὀξειῶν (sc. χορδῶν), like διὰ πασῶν, suggests a musician's term.

[2] In the modern senses of the terms.

[3] Cleonides also (207, 2 and 4 J) mentions πεττεία along with ἀγωγή and πλοκή as elements δι᾽ ὧν μελοποιία ἐπιτελεῖται. He adds a fourth, τονή (protraction of a note), while he defines πεττεία as ἡ ἐφ᾽ ἑνὸς τόνου πολλάκις γινομένη πλῆξις (repetition of a note). Bryennius (502 Wallis) follows the

ἢ γινώσκομεν τίνας μὲν τῶν φθόγγων ἀφετέον, τίνας δὲ παραληπτέον καὶ ὁσάκις ἕκαστον αὐτῶν καὶ ἀπὸ τίνος τε ἀρκτέον καὶ εἰς ὃν καταληκτέον· αὕτη δὲ καὶ τοῦ ἤθους γίνεται παραστατική. Nothing could be clearer. This department of composition takes the notes of the selected scale and by omissions and repetitions, by use of certain of them as initials and finals, produces the desired effect, which is, surely, a modal character, an ethos. The implication is that the system is not the whole story, the notes of the scale are but the draughts-pieces which the art of Petteia uses in the making of melody. The simple identification of the ethos-bearing modes with the species of the octave, which we found in (b), is thus considerably modified.

(d) 57, 29 ff., 58, 8 ff. Aristides, having found the sexual duality deeply rooted in the whole constitution of the world, is seeking to order the elements of music in the classes of male, female, and intermediate, with a view to applying the correct kinds of music in his psychotherapy. The notes of the basic scale are given characters corresponding to those of the vowels to which they were sung in the Greek "sol-fa" system. (These characters have just been described in II, ch. 13.) The characters of intervals (15 ff.) depend upon those of the notes, those of systems on those of the intervals, that compose them: (29 ff.) τῶν φθόγγων ἤτοι περιεχόντων, ἢ πλεοναζόντων, ἢ κατ' ἀμφότερα τὴν κυρίαν ἐχόντων, ἢ τῶν ἑτέρων καθ' ἕτερον τρόπον ὡς ἐν μίξει κατακρατούντων, τὰ ποιὰ γίνεται συστήματα, ἐκ δὲ τούτων αἱ ἁρμονίαι. That is to say, notes of differing character (this depending on their value in the Greater Perfect System) assert this character in any given system, either because they bound

account of Aristides, but conflates it (more suo) with that of Cleonides, adding τονή and its definition and inserting Cleonides's definition of πεττεία before that of Aristides. But the two are incompatible, despite the attempt of Bellermann (Anonymi Scriptio de Musica, p. 88) to reconcile them. We must choose between them; and that of Aristides is preferable, in that it explains the use of the word. Πεττεία was a game not closely resembling draughts, but involving the movement of pieces in accordance with a thought-out plan. Metaphors from it are common in Greek literature.

it[1] or occur frequently in it, or because they prevail in the re-
sultant mixture. Frequent occurrence in the system (e.g. the
diatonic F octave has three τη or pure female notes), not in
the melody, appears to be the point; for we are here dealing
with μίξις, not χρῆσις. The concluding words may be important: "and out of systems come the ἁρμονίαι". What relationship is envisaged between system and ἁρμονία? At first
sight it is attractive to take the latter in the sense of melody. But
this is inadmissible; ἁρμονία can only mean "melody" in the
sense of the whole melodic, as opposed to e.g. the rhythmical,
aspect of music. Probably Aristides means by systems the
minor consonances, and regards the ἁρμονίαι (here, as in
(b), simply the octaves) as made up of them. With this we can
compare the definitions of Thrasyllus already quoted:[2]
namely, of σύστημα as διαστημάτων ποιά περιοχή (cf.
Aristides 57, 16 περιεχόμενα), of ἁρμονία as συστημάτων
σύνταξις. The points of view are the same, and in either case,
if ἁρμονία simply equals octave-system, the definitions overlap;
the octave is both a system and a structure of subordinate
systems, which is perfectly true. But the relationship of
system to ἁρμονία is involved again in the next passage we
must consider.

After discussing for a few sentences the principles upon
which the treatment is to be applied, Aristides returns to the
former subject. Ἁρμονίαι, he says, resemble the intervals
that frequently in them or the notes that bound them,
and the notes, in their turn, resemble the motions and emo-
tions of the soul. As evidence for the influence of music (or
rather of notes in music) over character he quotes the school of
Damon (58, 13): "for instance in the ἁρμονίαι handed down
by him we find that of the movable-notes now the female,

---

[1] Aristides uses περιέχειν in two senses: "bound" and "compose". For the
latter see 10, 5; 10, 16; 57, 16. But that does not make sense here (or at 58, 8),
as it would afford no reasonable antithesis to πλεονάζειν. We should rather
compare 8, 19; 10, 20; 14, 10; (and especially) 10, 24 (systems "bounded" by
"standing-" or "movable-notes").

[2] P. 12.

now the male, occur with greater or less frequency or are even omitted entirely, clearly because the usefulness of the mode depends on the character of the particular soul. So it is that of all the departments of Melodic Composition that which is called Petteia is the most valuable, which is a question of selecting the notes essential on each occasion."[1] What ἁρμονίαι are these? It is hardly surprising that Meibom, in view of the mention of Petteia and the similarity of language to the passage that describes it in Book 1, wished to take ἁρμονίαι of melodies. But this, we have seen, is not admissible. Aristides must be referring to scales, and to gapped scales such as those he gives himself (1, ch. 9), the scales we considered in an earlier section. It is even arguable that it is to them that he is referring.[2] A discussion of this point or an attempt to relate the details of this sentence to the details of those scales would be out of place here. But, if these are scales, what is their relation to Petteia, which is concerned with melodies? It depends upon the point of διό. If Aristides was thinking logically, he must have meant: there are certain gapped scales, which by the particular notes they omit and employ[3] are the bases of melodies that produce certain effects on the soul; on a similar principle it is Petteia in actual composition that is the most powerful ethical agent, because it is continually selecting the proper notes for use and emphasis in each case. Yet I doubt if his mind was quite clear

---

[1] ἐν γοῦν ταῖς ὑπ' αὐτοῦ παραδεδομέναις ἁρμονίαις τῶν φερομένων φθόγγων ὁτὲ μὲν τοὺς θήλεις, ὁτὲ δὲ τοὺς ἄρρενας ἔστιν εὑρεῖν ἤτοι πλεονάζοντας ἢ ἐπ' ἔλαττον ἢ οὐδ' ὅλως παρειλημμένους, δῆλον ὡς κατὰ τὸ ἦθος ψυχῆς ἑκάστης καὶ ἁρμονίας χρησιμευούσης. διὸ καὶ τῶν μερῶν τῆς μελοποιίας ἡ καλουμένη πεττεία τὸ χρησιμώτατον, ἐν ἐκλογῇ τῶν ἀναγκαιοτάτων φθόγγων ἑκάστοτε θεωρουμένη. We know little of Damon except that he was the authority in whom Socrates in the *Republic* put his faith, and that he believed strongly in the ethical influence of music: a vague, but probably important, figure.

[2] To me this seems highly probable from a comparison of the phraseology of the two passages. Speaking of the ἁρμονίαι of less extent than an octave, he says (13, 11): οὐδὲ γὰρ πάντας παρελάμβανον ἀεὶ τοὺς φθόγγους (cf. οὐδ' ὅλως παρειλημμένους 58, 16). Compare also 14, 2–4 with 58, 16–17. This passage, in that case, is a fulfilment, not quite literal, of the promise at 14, 4.

[3] Why are only the movable-notes mentioned (58, 14)? Compare the mention of παρυπατοειδῆ and λιχανοειδῆ at 8, 13. Is it because these are the notes to which pure female (τη) and pure male (τω) characteristics are attached?

on the point.[1] There is a certain amount of confusion of
thought about scales and melodies, which does not show
itself only in Aristides; and it has an important bearing upon
the relation of system and ἁρμονία.

The confusion is perhaps best illustrated by the use of the
word μέλος to mean any succession of notes in music whether
in a scale sequence or in an actual melody. This is too
frequent to need the quotation of examples. It was suggested
by Clements (*JHS.* xlii (1922), 148–149) that the scales of
Aristides were "compass-scales", a stringing together of the
actual notes employed in a particular composition. Substi-
tute for "particular composition" "particular style of music",
and this becomes an illuminating way of regarding the old
modes. They are truly ἁρμονίαι, ways in which the strings of
the lyre must be tuned in order to play the desired kind of
music. As Athenaeus says (624 *d*), "the course of the melody
that the Dorians made they called the Dorian ἁρμονία". The
phrase used is τὴν ἀγωγὴν τῆς μελῳδίας; and, though we need
not suppose the word ἀγωγή is here used in a technical sense,
the connection between modal scale and modal song is well
brought out.[2] A scale is a kind of schematic representation of
mode; but scales may vary in abstraction. The old ἁρμονίαι
of the Greeks were the first stage of abstraction. A further was
to follow. For gradually theory develops, and the groups of
notes required for Dorian, Phrygian, Lydian music, and the
rest, are related together, the process ending in the highly
developed system of Aristoxenus with its basic scale analysed
into tetrachords, of which the species of the octave were

[1] I have omitted any mention of 57, 18–20, which raise difficulties, but do not
affect anything I have said above, merely illustrating the confusion further.
There ἡ τοῦ συστήματος ἀγωγή is contrasted with ἡ ὑπερβατὸς μελοποιία (*sic
codd. recte*). The latter expression must refer to actual composition, using πλοκή,
given earlier as a form of Melodic Composition (19, 19 ff., where the definition
of it includes the word ὑπερβατός). The former expression also presumably refers
to composition, that using ἀγωγή, that is, the natural order of the notes of the
scale (σύστημα). But the subject of the sentence seems to have fallen by the way.

I have also omitted to discuss the difficult καὶ συνεχοῦς μελῳδίας (καὶ is
wrongly omitted by Jahn, who was following MSS. without good authority) at
58, 11.

[2] I have avoided reference to the controversial question of the nature of the
Nomoi.

segments. For these theoretical scales the name of "system" came into use and ousted, for the theorists, the term ἁρμονία, which was less precise and attended with emotional associations.[1] This is the true relation of the terms, that of the notes of a melody or class of melodies, arranged in order, to those of a logical basic scale. But still confusion was not banished; partly, because μέλος could be applied to either or to the actual melody; partly, because the term ἁρμονία survived and was applied loosely to the octave-species, which were properly "systems" (though in some cases and perhaps to an increasing extent the notes of the sung melody and the octave-species may have been absolutely identical); partly, because the logic of Aristoxenian theory does not seem to have been fully sustained. Just as the Aristoxenians[2] illogically admitted Melodic Composition as a department of Harmonics, so in their analysis of systems they admit a subdivision into "continuous" and "gapped" (or "transilient": ὑπερβατά) systems, which seems designed to cover such scales as those of Aristides. The omissions of notes which went among other causes to produce the modal effects and should rightly have been included in the vague sphere of Melodic Composition (the Petteia of Aristides) are thus introduced even into the logical framework.[3]

The evidence of Aristides, if it is an orthodox amplification of Aristoxenus,[4] suggests that, if the old modalities were

[1] This is perhaps suggested by Plato, *Philebus*, 17 c–d. Cf. Aristoxenus 36, 30 M.
[2] See p. 54, n. 3.
[3] We can compare the double employment of the adjective ὑπερβατός in Aristides: (10, 8 and 36) of the gapped scale; (19, 25; 57, 19) of disjunct movement in an actual melody, which passes over degrees in the scale-sequence. At 58, 27 (where the reference is to systems) we should probably emend ὑπερβολῶν to ὑπερβατῶν, understanding φθόγγων from the previous line. The rather absurd expression ὑπερβατοὶ φθόγγοι can be paralleled from 10, 36; it is intelligible as a compression of φθόγγοι καθ' ὑπέρβασιν λαμβανόμενοι, which we find at 12, 7. Indeed Ptolemy uses it (67, 8 D: τῆς διὰ τῶν ὑπερβατῶν φθόγγων συμπλοκῆς).
[4] It is impossible to discuss the sources of Aristides here. Porphyry (125, 24 Düring) refers to a work of Aristoxenus περὶ μελοποιίας in at least four books, which may have been one of them. Deiters ("De Aristidis Q. doctrinae harmonicae fontibus", *Programm Gymn. Düren.* 1870) held that many passages in him are derived from the school of Damon in the fifth century. There is much to support this view, but lost works of Aristoxenus may have been the connecting link.

suppressed in the outward form of the latter's system, this suppression may have been more apparent than real. But, in fact, there is more than a possibility that Aristides is drawing upon older sources (transmitted, it may be, by Aristoxenus himself), and that what he says has more application to an earlier period. It is true that his object is, professedly, practical and one that would therefore be frustrated unless he was dealing with the music of his own time. But his doctrine of the educational and curative value of music is essentially an antiquarian revival; nor were his contemporaries at all likely to use his prescriptions (which are, when it comes to the point, exceedingly vague) for the benefit of their souls. There are then two drawbacks about the evidence of Aristides. Firstly, it is not proof positive that the subtleties of mode it implies had survived during the centuries that elapsed between the time of Damon and the date at which he wrote. On this, as on so many points in this exasperating subject, it is desirable to keep an open mind. Secondly, granted that what he says is true of all periods of Greek music, though it throws a fresh light upon the Aristoxenian system by suggesting that modal scales approximating to the octave-species must have been in the mind of the framer of it, he does not help us to decide whether these modal octaves came into the system merely through the doctrine of the species or were also fundamental to the conception of the τόνοι (thus retaining their connection with the modal names). That this was true of the τόνοι of Ptolemy is beyond doubt: it is his theoretical system that must next be examined.

§ 3. THE EVIDENCE OF PTOLEMY

Writing in the second century A.D., Ptolemy, a lucid thinker if an ungainly writer, expounds a system of Harmonics which makes a very different impression from that of the Aristo-xenians. For, though both of them contain τόνοι which are two-octave scales, Ptolemy makes it clear that the function of these is to be the bearers, as it were, of the species of the octave, so that their number is limited to seven. His tone is sometimes polemical, as though he were an innovator; but perhaps more often it is judicial, as though he were summing up controversies of long standing. It is clear at many points in his argument that he has in view an opposing theory in which the τόνοι were divorced from their connection with the octave-species, were in fact pitch-keys. These opponents we will describe as Aristoxenians. Spiritual descendants of Aristoxenus they were, since his work upon the τόνοι stands behind them, whether he himself realised to the full the implications of what he had done or not.

The question at issue appears in the form: what is the true nature of a τόνος? It might be put otherwise: who is to use the term τόνος, the Aristoxenians for their pitch-keys ranged at semitonal intervals or Ptolemy for his seven "keys", whose nature depends on the varying succession of intervals within them? It might appear to be a mere wrangle about terminology. It is saved from this, only if at this date the word τόνος, associated with the old modal names, was used, as ἁρμονία once had been and perhaps was still, to describe the significant units of Greek music, and if there was a theory of τόνοι which failed to correspond to this usage. We must examine the difference between the Aristoxenian and Ptolemaic conceptions of "key" in some detail. The following points emerge at different stages of Ptolemy's coherent and close-knit argument.

(i) II, chs. 4–5. The species of fourth, fifth, and octave have been enumerated (ch. 3). From early times the term "perfect" (τέλειον) had been applied to a system or systems. In Aristides it is the octave (10, 26 J, etc.); in Cleonides the Greater and Lesser Perfect Systems have the range of two octaves and an eleventh respectively.[1] Ptolemy refuses the title to any system of less than two octaves, but does not limit it to the "special case" of the double-octave that is the

---

[1] Bacchius (308, 3 J) gives the "conjunct" and "disjunct" perfect systems the range of an eleventh and a twelfth respectively: that is, the Greater Perfect System has been docked of the tetrachord Hyperbolaion. Cleonides, 200, 10 ff.

Greater Perfect System. His motives for this dictum are more important than his arguments: he wishes to base his theory of "keys" upon the species of the double-octave; and every species of it in fact fulfils his definition of perfection.[1] The notes of any such double-octave may be named (or identified) "by position" (κατὰ θέσιν), the middle note being Mese, the extremes Proslambanomenos and Nete Hyperbolaion, and so on. Alongside this (thetic) nomenclature "by position" exists the more familiar (dynamic) nomenclature "by function" (κατὰ δύναμιν), according to which a note in any double-octave can be described by its position in the Changeless System (σύστημα ἀμετάβολον), the Greater Perfect System of the Aristoxenians. Ptolemy might have put it thus:[2] that any perfect system is a section from a fixed, but theoretically illimitable, series of intervals (or, for him, ratios). But the only way that tradition had given him of describing them was by means of the Greater Perfect System, so that we are left with the difficulty of deciding what exactly is the balance of importance between the thetic and dynamic aspects of his system.

It is the thetic nomenclature[3] that is Ptolemy's novelty, and we can see the motive for its introduction. It is to supply a

[1] In dismissing the claims of the eleventh he remarks (51, 2 ff. D) that it does not contain all species of the octave *ever* or all of the fifth *always*; and he illustrates this from two species of this consonance.

[2] Cf. 101, 2 ff.: the series of notes is indefinitely extensible, but the number of different functions is limited. Thus Proslambanomenos of one cycle begins another as Nete Hyperbolaion. That it is a cycle of double and not single octaves is a result of the history of Greek music.

[3] Düring (*Ptolemaios und Porphyrios über die Musik*, p. 220) demurs to the expression ὀνομασία κατὰ θέσιν as applied to notes. But it is justified by 51, 20 ff. (τοὺς...φθόγγους...παρ' αὐτὴν τὴν θέσιν...ὀνομάζομεν); and Ptolemy himself uses this nomenclature at 75, 2, 4 (cf. 65, 2 ff.) to describe the limits of the central octave, in which the species are found. Further, Düring mistranslates 53, 10 ff.: Ptolemy does not say that the notes can only be rightly named according to the dynamic designations, but that they can only be called "standing" or "movable" according to it—for the reason that he gives in the following sentence, namely, that the τόποι (the degrees) of the thetic nomenclature do not keep the same description of note, "standing" or "movable", as the δυνάμεις change their θέσεις. Düring's discussion of chapter five contains much that is useful, but he goes too far in stressing the connection of the thetic nomenclature and the Grundskala. This criticism also applies to Abert's and Vetter's definitions of θέσις and δύναμις (Adler's *Handbuch der Musikgeschichte*, p. 34: *RE.* col. 829). See text, *infra*.

standard of comparison between his "keys". In the Aristoxenian scheme of pitch-keys the identical replicas of the
Greater Perfect System are simply related by the semitonal
steps at which they stand from one another. But the seven
"keys" of Ptolemy, covering roughly the same range of
(abstract) pitch and varying in the order of their intervals,
need some fixed frame of reference to relate their variations.
This is provided, we might say, in two stages: first, the
establishment of fifteen degrees or the taking of an instrument
of fifteen strings, having an order of pitch independent of any
actual tuning; secondly, the identification of these degrees or
strings by giving them the names they have when the instrument is tuned to the Changeless System. It is not always
tuned in this way; but the correspondence of θέσις and δύναμις
in the Dorian gives us a fixed standard by which to note the
aberrations of the others. It is probably true to say that the
thetic nomenclature was not intended to be, for all purposes,
an alternative way of naming notes alongside the dynamic.
At the same time it is misleading to stress too much the origin
of the thetic names. Θέσις is something that remains un-
changed in every species; and in an expression like ὁ τόπος
παρυπάτης μέσων it is the first member, not the second, that
is significant. Thus, though the use of traditional names gives
an apparent predominance to one species, it is a far more
essential fact that, being names of degrees (or strings),[1] they
apply equally to all species. In short, by his redefinition of a
Perfect System and the application of a standard nomenclature to all the species of the double-octave, Ptolemy has in
effect deprived the Greater Perfect System of its pre-
eminence. But this discussion has caused us to anticipate and
to assume the nature of the Ptolemaic "keys" before tracing
the process that arrives at them, in the course of which further
interesting points arise.

[1] Reinach puts it well (*La musique grecque*, p. 61 n.): "ces noms n'ont que la
valeur de simples numéros d'ordre". It is to be noted that, since Mese, Lichanos,
etc., were originally names of *strings*, which had become associated with a particular tuning, this is a reversion to an earlier usage.

66   THE EVIDENCE OF PTOLEMY

(ii) Ch. 6. The Aristoxenians had given the title of "perfect" to that system also that contained the tetrachord Synemmenon. Ptolemy, arguing from the premises of his opponents,[1] shows that the effect of the inclusion of this tetrachord is to give a transitory modulation of key at the fourth. But such a modulation is rightly distinguished by Aristoxenian theorists from a normal modulation of key and called a modulation of system. For there are two kinds of modulation of τόνος (that is, modulations that involve the transposition of a series of notes to a different pitch): one is a mere repetition of the whole scale (or μέλος) at a higher or lower pitch; in the other, part of it remains the same, but part abandons the original consecution (τὴν ἐξαρχῆς ἀκολουθίαν 55, 3) and by frustrating the expectation of the listener produces a sense of change affecting the ethos (φαντασία ἑτερότητος τῆς κατὰ τὴν δύναμιν ὑφ' ἧς κινεῖται τὸ ἦθος 55, 7). The pitch indeed changes (there is a modulation of key at the fourth), but the object is not a change of pitch for its own sake, but a change of melodic character.[2] For Pto-

---

[1] Ptolemy's argument is freely restated in the text with the help of Aristoxenian terminology. It is essential to the understanding of this chapter to realise that Ptolemy is thinking in terms of (a) pitch-keys, (b) the classification of modulations we find in Cleonides (of Genus, of Key, of System—while that of Melodic Composition, with its association with ethos, is also at the back of his mind). First he distinguishes modulations of γένος and τόνος (54, 9); then points out that there are two types of modulation that involve τόνος, but treat it very differently. It is clear that he is arguing from Aristoxenian premises from the fact that he calls simple transposition (54, 13 f.) a modulation of τόνος (55, 4), whereas his own μεταβολή κατὰ τὸν τόνον (58, 9) is more like the μεταβολή κατὰ σύστημα of the Aristoxenians: i.e. τοῦ μέλους μᾶλλον ἢ τοῦ τόνου μεταβολή (cf. 55, 6 with 58, 7 ff.); for both produce φαντασία ἑτερότητος κ.τ.λ. (cf. 55, 7 and 20 with 58, 20). Τόνος then, in this chapter, is used in the sense of a repetition of the same series of notes at a different pitch (τάσις, in fact, in a further dimension: cf. 57, 16). This explains the expression ὁ οὕτω λεγόμενος τόνος at 54, 12 and again at 57, 16: it means τόνος as pitch-key as opposed to the sense it is to bear later. (Düring's suggestion that τόνος in 54, 11 and 12 means disjunctive tone is quite unacceptable: (a) it must mean the same thing in these places as at 55, 4, where Düring translates it "Tonhöhe"; (b) 54, 12 and 57, 16 must be interpreted together; (c) the δύναμις of the disjunctive tone is always one and the same and not susceptible to μεταβολή; the paraphrase "die Lage der diazeuktischen Ganztöne" (Düring, op. cit. p. 230) exposes the weakness of the interpretation.) As I have taken it, καί in 54, 12 means "in fact", παρά means "deriving their name from" (cf. 57, 14; 62, 20).

[2] 55, 6: ἡ δὲ τάσις οὐχ ὡς τάσις ἀλλ' ὡς ἕνεκα τοῦ μέλους (sc. ἀλλάσσεται).

THE EVIDENCE OF PTOLEMY

lemy, a true modulation must produce such an impression of change, or, as he puts it later, ἐξαλλαγή καὶ πλάνη ταῖς αἰσθήσεσι τοῦ γενομένου παρὰ τὸ προσδοκηθέν; and among the Aristoxenian varieties of modulation he finds this in those of genus and system, not in that of key. Thus this apparent digression on the Lesser Perfect System has taught us what Ptolemy will demand of a "key" and has enabled him to make an essential criticism of a rival system. We may put it in this way: a system whose central feature was pitch-keys did not account for the differences of character or ethos which Ptolemy felt were an important part of Greek music; modulation of "system" covered but a part of the ground; most was relegated to the department of Melodic Composition, which was not, strictly considered, a part of harmonic theory at all; Ptolemy's own system of τόνοι will take into account these differences of ethos.

(iii) Ch. 7. He begins with the statement that transpositions of complete systems (καθ' ὅλας τὰς συστάσεις) are potentially infinite, since there are infinite degrees of pitch. (Are Ptolemy's τόνοι then to be simply transpositions?) In actual aesthetic fact (57, 20) they are limited; and Ptolemy limits them, as we shall see, to seven, the number of ratios in the octave. If they had been pure pitch-keys, there would have been no need for such a limitation. But Ptolemy criticises those who make the scope of voices or instruments their standard, and lays down the principle that τόνοι do not exist for the purpose of obtaining higher and lower sounds; if that is desired, then retune the whole instrument or get fresh singers.[1] What then is the true purpose of a τόνος? It is explained in difficult language, as though Ptolemy were struggling with the inadequacies of existing terminology (as

---

[1] 58, 7 ff.: οὐδὲ γὰρ ἕνεκεν τῶν ὀξυτέρων ἢ βαρυτέρων φωνῶν εὕροιμεν ἂν τὴν σύστασιν τῆς κατὰ τὸν τόνον μεταβολῆς γεγενημένην—ὅποτε πρὸς τὴν τοιαύτην διαφορὰν ἢ τῶν ὀργάνων ὅλων ἐπίτασις ἢ πάλιν ἄνεσις ἀπαρκεῖ, μηδεμιᾶς γε παραλλαγῆς περὶ τὸ μέλος ἀποτελουμένης, ⟨ἢ⟩ ὅταν ὅλον ὁμοίως ὑπὸ τῶν βαρυφωνοτέρων ἢ τῶν ὀξυφωνοτέρων ἀγωνιστῶν διαπεραίνηται. I think ἢ must be supplied before ὅταν, the ὅταν clause being then an alternative subject to ἀπαρκεῖ; voice and instrument must be contrasted here, as by the μήτε–μήτε above (ll. 5–7).

indeed he was, if he was trying to make explicit the nature of modal differences). The object of a change of τόνος is to produce "a shift of ethos" (58, 14: τροπήν τινα τοῦ ἤθους) or "an impression of a different ethos" (58, 20: ἑτέρου ἤθους φαντασίαν) in the following manner.[1] The range of the voice is occupied by a series of intervals, the μέλος; when a change of τόνος occurs, the limits of the voice and of the μέλος no longer correspond, and a group of intervals that was formerly in the upper part of the range may now be in the lower. In effect, the fixed, but extensible, series of intervals moves on a sliding scale against the range of the voice. If that range be (roughly) two octaves, then in each mutation of τόνος it will be occupied by a different species of the double-octave, or Perfect System; but this is not made clear till ch. 11.

(iv) Ch. 11. Ptolemy has enumerated his seven τόνοι and explained their disposition. That their (non-inclusive) limit is the octave has already been argued in ch. 8; now he demonstrates that it is inadmissible to add more within the octave. In one aspect his τόνοι can be regarded as Aristoxenian keys on seven degrees of pitch. But they are without the strict spatial limitations of Aristoxenian keys; or rather, they are limited in a different fashion, for they extend roughly along the two-octave limit of a single voice or instrument. Each of them is then a Perfect System, not, like the Aristoxenian key, a replica of the Changeless System, but each a different species of the double-octave. It is significant that Aristoxenians compare τόνοι by the relations of their Proslambanomenoi, Ptolemy by the relations of their Mesai.[2] Take the central octave of each, from Nete Diezeugmenon to

---

[1] Düring seems to distinguish two processes in ll. 13–20. But the double reference to change of ethos at 15 and 20 makes it clear that there is only one; πῆ μὲν ἀπολεῖπον κ.τ.λ. is a restatement of ἀεὶ προκαταλήγειν κ.τ.λ. Further, τὸ ἐξαρχῆς ἐφαρμόσαν τῇ διαστάσει τῆς φωνῆς (cf. 55, 3) may be any perfect system: it *may* be the Grundskala, which makes a convenient standard and is used as such in the thetic nomenclature.

[2] To relate Ptolemaic τόνοι by their Proslambanomenoi leads to an inelegant demonstration, as some of them are below, some above the central octave. This is what Aristides does in 15, 11 ff. J (see p. 51, n. 5).

Hypate Meson by the thetic nomenclature, and in each case Mese "by function" falls on a different thetic degree.[1] As there are only seven degrees upon which Mese can fall (the eighth is a mere repetition at the octave), there can only be seven τόνοι; any others will be otiose, merely duplicating one of the existing τόνοι a semitone higher or lower. We now see that, just as the total range manifests the species of the double-octave, so the central octave manifests those of the octave; and this is the true significance of Ptolemy's system of τόνοι.[2] For it is the central region of the voice that is most used in melody, and the modes whose existence is implied throughout Ptolemy's argument were equivalent to the species of the octave; and it is these that form the lyre and cithara scales that he mentions in the last chapter of the book.[3]

To sum up, the modes of the early period were in many ways anomalous, but were ultimately systematised as the seven species of the octave. Aristides and Ptolemy are alike in suggesting that these octave-systems continued to be the basis of Greek music; and, though the antiquarianism of Aristides makes him but doubtful evidence for later times, there can be no doubt that Ptolemy is speaking of contemporary music. Aristides further suggests that by suitable treatment of the notes of these octave-scales it was possible to reproduce the characteristics of the old modes. Unfortunately, the light that Ptolemy throws upon the details of the modes is but slight. We have seen how he labours in describing the nature of modal differences. In both chs. 6 and 7 a shift of character, caused by a defeat of the expectation of the listener, is demanded as the mark of a real modulation; but

---

[1] Cf. Aristides 11, 14 f. J.

[2] It is impossible to bring the species of both the double and the single octave within the same range of pitch in the same scheme. Ptolemy chooses the single octave, with the result that the limits of his Hypolydian τόνος are a semitone higher than those of the others. This choice is significant of the real bearing of his system.

[3] 80, 12: οἱ ἀπὸ νήτης τοῦ τονιαίου διατόνου ἀριθμοὶ κ.τ.λ.. (with reference to the tables in the preceding chapter).

all we are told of the means by which this is brought about
is that there is a discrepancy between the limits of the voice
and the series of intervals that originally occupied it. Later
this is shown to mean, in effect, that the central octave of the
voice is occupied now by one octave-species, now by another.
But nothing is said to indicate that the varying character of
these depended upon the different modal values of the notes
in them. There is only one standard of "value", in Ptolemy
as in other Greek theorists, that of the Changeless System.
It is this, and in particular its Mese, that is used as a means
of comparison of his τόνοι; it is this even that gives the names
to that scheme of degrees (the thetic nomenclature) that is
common to all of them. Yet the general trend of his system is,
as we have seen, towards the diminution of its pre-eminence
and the equality of all the τόνοι. We might conclude that in
these the extremes, which form, as it were, the pivots of the
whole structure, were of modal importance. But we must then
ask whether we must consider the extremes of the double or
single octaves. The argument is based for the most part upon
the former, and the significance of the central octave of the
τόνος does not appear till a late stage and then not very
explicitly. Yet the species of the double-octave cannot have
been the basis of practical music. Ch. 15 does not help us
much. There the figures for the relative string-lengths of notes,
in each τόνος, in several different intonations, are given in
two separate octaves, descending from thetic Nete Diezeugmenon and Mese respectively. The only conceivable bearing
that this could have on mode would be the suggestion that in
each octave not only the extremes were modally important,
but also the fourth note from the bottom (the note corresponding to the extremes of the double-octave). This would
indeed support an interpretation of a passage in the Aristotelian Problems examined and rejected above.[1] But there is

---

[1] Note that the case for thetic Mese as a universal tonic rests on the least
plausible interpretation of Ar. Prob. xix, 20 (pp. 5 f.), on incomplete
illustration by the fragments (p. 46), and on this procedure of Ptolemy, which
can be otherwise accounted for.

a simpler explanation. Ptolemy wished to demonstrate the series of ratios as completely as possible. But two-octave diagrams would be not only clumsy, but unrelated to practice. The essential thing was to give the figures for the central octave. For the rest of the τόνος the octave either above or below thetic Mese would suffice.

But, if Ptolemy gives us little or no information about actual modalities, his evidence is invaluable for the survival of mode. And the modes in Ptolemy are in effect the τόνοι, and, as such, still retain connection with the old names of the ἁρμονίαι. But between ἁρμονίαι and Ptolemaic τόνοι lie many centuries, and Aristoxenus. We must return to the subject of the first section of this chapter, must ask what is the correct interpretation of the τόνοι of Aristoxenus, and must consider the implications of the answer, whatever it may be.

§ 4. MODE AND KEY

The conception of τόνος passed through two phases. In the first the τόνοι were the means of relating modal octaves in the same range of pitch by representing them as segments of a uniform scale repeated at different degrees of pitch. In the second these repetitions of the uniform scale took on an independent existence as keys in the modern sense. The second phase was clearly reached as a development of the first. The question we must now consider is at what stage this development took place: in particular, whether the work of Aristoxenus represents the culmination of the first phase, the beginning of the second, or (a third possibility) a stage of transition. The somewhat confusing indications must be briefly reviewed.

(i) The achievement of Aristoxenus in this line was to put an end to the confusion that had existed previously (37, 8 ff.). This confusion was probably caused, partly, by the anomalous constructions of the old modes, partly, by vagueness as to what constituted a pitch relation between scales. But to

perform this feat it was only necessary to perfect the first phase
of the τόνοι, when once the modes had been systematised as
the octave-species.

(ii) The fact that the Proslambanomenoi of his τόνοι are
limited by the octave and the absence of evidence that he
departed from the names of the octave-species allow us to
believe that his keys were integrally connected with these
species.

(iii) One of the principles adopted by his predecessors in
the arrangement of τόνοι was the so-called καταπύκνωσις (7,
2; 38, 2). The details of this process are obscure, but it seems
to have been, like a scheme of pitch-keys, an attempt to map
out and account for a gamut of sound. This principle Aristoxenus criticises adversely. Again, if the conception of pitch-
keys was stimulated or even necessitated by the auloi (cf.
p. 50) and closely linked to the notation, it is noteworthy
that he expressly (39, 4 ff.) deprecates making either the
notation of melodies or the theory of the aulos the end and
object of harmonics.

(iv) However, it appears from the subsequent discussion
that he is thinking of writers who treated musical theory
empirically on a basis of the technique of that instrument. It
certainly does not follow that, because he criticised them, he
was uninfluenced in his outlook by the aulos, which is the
only instrument he mentions; and, if he knew of families of
extensive auloi giving two-octave chromatic scales,[1] they
might have encouraged in him the idea of τόνοι as replicas
and helped him towards the semitonal distribution of them.
Nor, because he disparages καταπύκνωσις, did he necessarily
make no concession to it.

(v) Clearly the aim described in (i) demands the existence
of seven τόνοι only. What then was his motive for adding the

---

[1] The earlier type of aulos could only play the scale of one particular mode,
but by the time of Aristoxenus auloi were of extensive compass and distinguished
not by the modes they could play but by their general range of pitch (cf. Aristoxenus 20, 32 ff. and ap. Athen. 634 e). The evidence for two octaves of semitones
is in Aristotle, Met. 1093 b 2.

intervening τόνοι, then or later called Ionian, Aeolian, etc.? If his τόνοι were integrally associated with the octave-species, then the point of these intervening τόνοι must have been to provide certain of the species in two varieties, higher and lower. What was the value of this? The difference in pitch is negligible for any purpose. Nor is there in most cases a practical advantage to the string-player in greater simplicity of tuning.[1] Even supporters of this view question the practical significance of these additional keys. But, if this was not his motive, he can only have made the additions in order to map out the gamut more completely and has by his semitonal arrangement made a kind of concession to καταπύκνωσις.[2] As τόνοι of the first phase they have little object, as τόνοι of the second they marshal the tonal space more neatly; and Aristoxenus's linear conception of scales would make him peculiarly susceptible to their appeal.

(vi) Unfortunately, we possess no systematic treatment of the topic by him; and his isolated remarks upon it are not very precise. The point that emerges most clearly is the connection between τόνοι and modulation (7, 22 ff.; 38, 6 ff.). Ptolemy also demands that the τόνοι shall be so placed as to facilitate modulation; and modulation for him involves a change of species or mode. But he refers also to a type of modulation that transposes a whole series of notes, which is modulation of key in the modern sense. Aristoxenus may have been referring to this, for which also a certain disposition of keys is desirable. However, in the latter of the passages referred to, he speaks of modulation as a modification in the melodic *order* (πάθους...συμβαίνοντος ἐν τῇ τῆς μελῳδίας τάξει). But the melodic order does not change from pitch-key to pitch-key, whereas such a change, such a πάθος is

---

[1] The Hypolydian needs the tuning up of five strings, the low Hypolydian or Hypoaeolian (on this hypothesis) the tuning down of three only; the Lydian octave can be obtained either by raising or by lowering four strings.

[2] Laloy, *op. cit.* p. 250: "c'est là une application ingénieuse, mais modérée et raisonnée, de cette subdivision des diagrammes, que les précurseurs d'Aristoxène avaient inventée et poussée à l'extrême."

what Ptolemy demands of a modulation of τόνος. Again, Aristoxenus speaks (7, 11 ff.) of the important differences of melody that result from placing identical systems in particular ranges of pitch. It is hard to believe that he is thinking merely of a difference of pitch; we are rather reminded of Ptolemy's attempts to describe modal distinctions (see pp. 67 f.).

These considerations are hardly enough to settle the matter beyond doubt. The words of Aristoxenus suggest that he had in mind the original connection between τόνος and octave-species. But his action in adding the intervening τόνοι seems to belie his words. We can scarcely acquit him of confusion of thought in any case (and Ptolemy would allow no plea for mercy). He stands at the point of transition from phase to phase, and his τόνοι hover uneasily between the two conceptions. But one or the other must have been uppermost in his mind. Let us adopt either hypothesis in turn and consider its implications.

(1) We may believe that the thirteen τόνοι of Aristoxenus were not pitch-keys, but, like those of Ptolemy, essentially "retunings" (ἁρμονίαι, μεθαρμογαί).[1] In that case the polemic of Ptolemy cannot be simply against Aristoxenus himself. It must have a double objective: it must be directed partly against Aristoxenus, whose six otiose τόνοι (including the Hypermixolydian) were a betrayal of the essential basis of such a system of τόνοι, partly against those theorists who added pitch-keys beyond the octave. These theorists may be regarded as descendants of Aristoxenus, in that they pursued to its conclusion a path along which he had taken only one step, by the addition of the otiose τόνοι. By what stages and how rapidly this (hypothetical) progress was made, we are no longer in a position to say.[2] But, if Ptolemy (II, ch. 6) has been rightly interpreted above, it would appear that he took

[1] Cf. Phrynichus in Bekk. *Anecd.* I 15, 29 (quoted by Düring, *op. cit.* p. 237), who equates τόνοι and ἁρμονίαι and speaks of thirteen of the latter.
[2] Nor do we know at what stage began the use of the Aeolian and Ionian names, which symbolises the detachment of τόνοι from species. But see p. 19, n. 2.

the μεταβολὴ κατὰ τόνον of the manuals to be modulation of *key*. This leads us to the conclusion that the Aristoxenians were perhaps less purely Aristoxenian than they have sometimes been thought to be.

(2) If, on the other hand, the τόνοι of Aristoxenus were primarily pitch-keys, we must account for the phrases quoted above in (vi) as reversions to the earlier conception, the implications of which were disregarded by him in the framing of his system. We have also to account for the appearance of the earlier conception in Ptolemy. It is unlikely to have been an innovation of his own. We know from him that the Aristoxenian system of τόνοι was not the only one in the field. In particular, there was a school of thought that accepted eight τόνοι only, disposed like those of Ptolemy with the addition of the Hypermixolydian. Ptolemy criticises these theorists (62, 16ff. D) for their method of procedure and cannot accept their eighth τόνος; but their limitation of the τόνοι to eight makes it probable that their attitude towards them was "Ptolemaic". Unfortunately, we are given no indication of their date. The period between Aristoxenus and Ptolemy remains an almost complete blank. Plutarch will not help us to fill it; for the treatise standing under his name is of doubtful authenticity and (therefore) date. It is however significant that the terms ἁρμονία and τόνος (or τρόπος) seem there to be used interchangeably in the sense of mode.[1] The inference to be drawn is that the τόνος, with modal name attached, was the significant unit of the music of the time. Yet at that very same date melodies must have been noted in the Dorian, Phrygian, Hypolydian and other pitch-keys and were presumably describable as in these keys. Thus there must have been two divergent employments of the names and of

---

[1] For Plutarch's usage see Monro, *op. cit.* pp. 20ff. Cf. especially § 366 and Arist. *Pol.* viii, 1342 *b* 9. The history of τρόπος, which through the Latin *modus* gives us our "mode", is obscure. Its technical use cannot be established in any author before Dionysius of Halicarnassus, who uses it in the sense of "mode" (*de comp. verb.* 19). It appears as a synonym for τόνος in the manuals, where it is actually the commoner of the two terms.

the term τόνος simultaneously in use, corresponding to the two phases of development of the τόνοι. Again we are faced with alternative hypotheses.

(i) We may believe that the term τόνος had come into use during the confusion before Aristoxenus in a sense practically indistinguishable from that of ἁρμονία,[1] and continued so to be used, at least popularly, during the whole period between then and Ptolemy, whose work would thus be the culmination of a long tradition. We have already seen (p. 50) that this conception of τόνος is all that is required for the simpler types of music, particularly for that of the lyre. The divergences of theory could then be accounted for by a difference in point of view. One writer was thinking mainly in terms of wind-instruments, the other mainly in terms of strings; and the different conceptions of τόνος are natural to the respective instruments. It was natural for the string-player to think of modes in terms not of absolute pitch, but of the varying orders of intervals according as the instrument was tuned and then retuned.[2] The auloi, however, were extensive, and distinguished by the different pitches at which they were graded, which must have suggested the idea of identical scales graded in a similar way. Each school of thought would thus use τόνος in the sense appropriate to it; and the two uses would co-exist. But there is a corollary to this. Such a difference of point of view might well affect theory. But the actual music played upon aulos and cithara cannot have differed so widely; indeed they were often played together in unison. Thus, if one preserved modal distinctions, the other must have preserved them also. It follows that the submergence of modal variety, which the transference of the modal names to a system of pitch-keys suggests, must have been more apparent than real.

[1] Cf. Laloy, *Aristoxène*, pp. 123 ff.
[2] At first the τόνοι bring the seven species within the same range. This suffices for the lyre; and notes lying above and below the central octave can be disregarded for practical purposes. The greater number of strings on the cithara enabled melodies to exceed the octave (as many of the surviving melodies do), and thus led to Ptolemy's view of the τόνοι as retunings of a double-octave, of which nevertheless the central octave is the (modally important) kernel.

(ii) There is a second hypothesis: namely, that the use of τόνος for "mode" is subsequent to Aristoxenus and perhaps caused in part by the assumption of the modal names by keys that were essentially different from modes. The history of the term would then be as follows. The τόνοι were at first a device for relating the octave-species within the same range of pitch, and as such bore the names of the latter. But they developed into pitch-keys, retaining the modal names; and for the time these keys were the significant units of Greek music. When, later, music became predominantly modal once more, the names returned to the modes and brought with them the term τόνος (and such phrases as ἐπὶ τόνου...τίθεσθαι, which are really inappropriate to the idea of mode). This hypothesis presents us with a difficult picture, but one that becomes intelligible as we inspect it. First modal variety; then key displacing mode; then modal variety again. It is intelligible on two assumptions: first, that there was for a period a notable submergence of mode; secondly, that this was submergence and not disappearance (i.e. we must account for the reappearance, at some stage, of modal variety).

Key and mode are to some extent mutually antagonistic. The badge of mode is idiosyncrasy, of key uniformity; and keys cannot be established unless there is some standard of reference. So in Greek music modes could not be related in a system of τόνοι until they were conceived as parts of a fundamental series of notes and intervals. This in itself implies a measure of standardisation. But it implies the weakening of trenchant modal characters rather than the submergence of modal variety. The music that lay behind the theoretical system of Ptolemy was standardised in this way, but it was (if we are right) still modal. But there is another aspect of Greek theory that implies standardisation in still greater measure. It is the analysis of the fundamental scale into tetrachords and the doctrine of the variation of the genera within those tetrachords. For, if some notes are "standing-notes", while others can move according to genus within a considerable locus, it is hard to see how this can fail to give emphasis to the "standing-notes" and so to impose on all music that makes use of this variation a flavour that can justly be described as Dorian; for the structure of the Greater Perfect System is but an extension of the structure of the Dorian octave. Of other parts of the Aristoxenian system we may say that they distort or conceal the truth in the interests of symmetry. But, if the doctrine of the genera corresponded to reality at all, it can hardly signify anything but what has just been described. Ptolemy also discusses the genera at length.[1] But there is an important difference in the circumstances in which the two theorists wrote. In the time of Aristoxenus the enharmonic may have been almost obsolete, but the chromatic survived. Whereas, though Ptolemy gives his own version of the enharmonic and two types of chromatic, we learn from him that the enharmonic and the "soft" chromatic were no longer in use; and the one type of chromatic that he found in practice is almost identical with the "soft" diatonic of Aristoxenus.[2] We can consider then that the music of Ptolemy's era was almost purely diatonic and that any check that "modulation of genus" may have placed upon certain modalities had been largely removed. The fragments, as far as they go, fit into the picture. The later pieces are (apart from certain anomalies) purely diatonic. The only musical document that illustrates a normal use of the chromatic is the second Delphic hymn;[3] and the Delphic hymns, whose remoteness from Aristoxenus is to be measured in generations rather than in centuries, bear the stamp of standardisation (pp. 37 f.).

---

[1] And considers it worth while to point out which of the species of the consonances are bounded by "standing-notes": 49, 19 ff.; 53, 10 ff. D.

[2] Cf. *ClQu.* xxvi (1932), p. 205, n. 1. The use of διάτονος as a shortened form of expression for διάτονος λιχανός is fairly common. It is perhaps significant that Aristides should use it in describing the limits of the modal octaves (11, 11 and 13 J), thus showing that he thought of them in diatonic form only. In either case λιχανοῦ in Jahn's text is an emendation of his own. Cf. Bacchius 309, 9 f. J.

[3] The enharmonic of the *Orestes* papyrus does not help us.

The modes that lie behind Ptolemy's system are presumably those of the late diatonic melodies that have survived. The music of this era was diatonic and modal: that of the early period modal, but diatonic, chromatic, and enharmonic, though certainly not with the precision, deadly to mode, of Aristoxenian theory. Assuming that there was a hiatus of some kind, what reason have we to relate the two sets of modalities? Primarily, the stark improbability that a whole variety of new musical dialects could have developed or been imported at so late a stage of a country's music. They are then the same or similar modes, that have suffered temporary (and perhaps only partial) eclipse. It is a phenomenon for which only one hypothesis will account: namely, that the standardisation was a predominantly academic movement, powerful perhaps among the professors and the virtuosi; that all the time in the simpler forms of music and among the people the old modes, particularly in their diatonic forms, had continued to live, and, when first the enharmonic, then the chromatic, waned in popularity, once more held undisputed sway. Thus and thus only is it possible to account for what may be thought to be the facts.

But these facts are themselves only hypothetical. We have put forward a number of hypotheses: that the τόνοι of Aristoxenus were, like those of Ptolemy, in essence modes; that they were in essence pitch-keys, but that the implications of this in the way of standardisation of mode were illusory; that they were pitch-keys and represent a stage in Greek music at which mode had been, as it were, driven underground, only to reappear, when the factors that had led to this were themselves eliminated. Can we proceed a step further and select among these hypotheses one that seems more likely to be true than the others? I fear that our evidence will not allow us to do so. Thus we return to the situation that confronted us in dealing with Aristotelian Problem xix, 20 at the end of the first chapter. There, we were given the choice of believing that the ascription to Mese (κατὰ δύναμιν) of an importance perhaps amounting to the function of a tonic was the result either of a limitation in the interest of the writer or of a standardisation of modality in actual contemporary practice. Here also, one of the available hypotheses suggests such standardisation at the same period; and thus far the two interpretations support one another. Indeed some degree of standardisation there almost certainly was; but whether it went so far that it was reflected in the theoretical system of Aristoxenus and coloured the history of the τόνοι is another question, and one that can hardly be answered yes or no.

CONCLUDING NOTE

THE READER who has read so far will have seen that no very definite conclusions can be based upon this evidence. It is possible however to make a few statements about the Greek modes that are either certainly or probably true. The matter must be treated historically. At least up to the fifth century B.C. (and probably the fourth) Greek music knew many styles of melodies differing in emotional character and named after Hellenic or barbarian tribes. The notes required for each constituted a ἁρμονία, or tuning of the lyre. We have little evidence for the forms of these; but such as we have suggests considerable diversity, and it may not have been easy to combine them in a logical scale-system, or possible without sacrifice of their individualities. In particular, we are ignorant about the early history of the diatonic, chromatic, and enharmonic genera, and the extent to which any mode could use all three impartially. About the modal importance of the various notes in them we have practically no evidence independent of later developments: the one musical relic of this period is all too fragmentary. Yet this was the music of Sappho, Pindar, and the tragedians, in which our interest is naturally greatest.

Centuries later, the nature of Ptolemy's theoretical system is fairly clear. Seven τόνοι provided melodies which, like the ἁρμονίαι, differed in character; and these τόνοι were modes, being in essence species of the octave. Ptolemy offers no information about the relative values of their notes; for all he says we might believe that Mese (κατὰ δύναμιν) acted as tonic in each of them. Here the fragments come to our help. The information to be extracted from them has been summarised on p. 44 above. But, though they reveal diversity of mode, the number of different modalities that they illustrate with clarity is not enough to enable us to generalise from

them; they neither prove nor disprove the validity of any of
the neat schemes of tonics that have been postulated for the
Greek modes. Such as they are, can we use them as evidence
for the modes of an earlier day? Certainly the rich emotional
associations of a less sophisticated music had been lost;
certainly both theory and practice had reduced the anomalies
of the old modes to order; certainly all but diatonic intonations had been practically eliminated, a fact which may well
have affected the nature of all melody. Still there appears to
be an unbroken tradition between the ἁρμονίαι and Ptolemy's τόνοι. For the species of the octave are his inheritance
from earlier theorists and have their place in the system of
Aristoxenus also. And it is clear that they were to some
degree the heirs of the ἁρμονίαι, for both the term ἁρμονία
and the modal names were at some time applied to them.
How much they had lost, how much they transmitted to
Hellenistic and later music of the classical styles, how much
that was new developed in the course of centuries, can hardly
even be conjectured; and examination of the theory of
Aristoxenus and his followers throws but little light.

For it is mainly by the symmetrical bulk of this structure
that the hiatus between the ἁρμονίαι of Plato's *Republic* and
the τόνοι of Ptolemy is filled for us. It was intended to give
a theoretical basis to the music that Aristoxenus knew: its
realistic purpose is beyond question. If we could infer from it
the nature of that music, it would go some way to compensate
for the lack of musical documents. But we are met at once by
a difficulty. The species of the octave are indeed enumerated
by Aristoxenian writers, but it is implied that they ceased at
some stage to carry the modal names. Those names now
belong to the τόνοι, which form the principal feature of
Aristoxenus's system, as of Ptolemy's. There are however not
seven of them, but thirteen (later fifteen); and they are
disposed at regular intervals of a semitone. Now it is certain
that these τόνοι served as pitch-keys in connection with the
notation, and as such had lost their connection with the

octave-species. The question therefore arises whether or not Aristoxenus conceived his τόνοι as in intimate connection with the species: that is to say, whether or not they are, like Ptolemy's, essentially modal. Further, if they are not, does this imply that the music for which they were intended to account was more standardised in modality than that which preceded and followed it? The scanty and elusive evidence on these points has been examined in the last chapter. There are some considerations that suggest that Greek music may have passed through a stage of such standardisation: the varieties of the genera must have exerted an influence in this direction; the Delphic Hymns may provide an illustration of such standardised music; the one definite pronouncement of an ancient author upon the subject of modality is most simply interpreted as implying it. On the other hand, there are words of Aristoxenus that suggest that he was aware of a connection between his τόνοι and the species; the equation of τόνος and ἁρμονία may have begun far earlier than is vouched for by our evidence; and, finally, the modes, if they were to reappear in the forefront of theory, must have survived in practice, somewhere and in some degree.

In this inconclusive state we must leave the matter. Not even the main course of development of Greek music, far less the full details of its modalities, can be established on the evidence. It is a result to give rise to pessimism; and the prospects of further advances in our knowledge are not bright. We need actual pieces of music; and, though papyrus and stone will doubtless continue to give them to us, they will in all probability be as late, brief, and mutilated as those we already possess. Yet complete despondency is as unnecessary as it is ignoble. Every student of the subject must from time to time have the feeling that there is a certain amount of evidence, particularly concerning the earlier stages of Greek music, that is still unrelated together, and must hope that one day he will strike upon the true, the illuminating hypothesis which is to relate it. Meantime there is much work to be done before a new history of the art, a new "Gevaert" is due: new editions of some of the principal ancient authorities,[1] a critical examination of the historical information to be found in Plutarch, Athenaeus, and elsewhere, and a large number of special studies.

[1] Aristoxenus we already have, admirably edited by Macran; Ptolemy and Porphyry no less admirably edited by Düring. The present writer has in preparation an edition of Aristides Quintilianus. Perhaps the greatest need is for a fresh text of Plutarch's treatise (cf. Wilamowitz, *Griechische Verskunst*, p. 76, n. 3).

DIAGRAM

	Proslambanomenos	Hypate Hypaton	Parhypate Hypaton	Lichanos Hypaton	Hypate Meson	Parhypate Meson	Lichanos Meson	Mese	Paramese	Trite Diezeugmenon	Paranete Diezeugmenon	Nete Diezeugmenon	Trite Hyperbolaion	Paranete Hyperbolaion	Nete Hyperbolaion
Greater Perfect System = Changeless System of Ptolemy	A*	B*	c	d	e*	f	g	a*	b*	cl	dl	el*	fl	gl	al*
(Hypermixolydian)	(A	B	c	d	e	f	g	a)							
Mixolydian		B	c	d	e	f	g	a	b						
Lydian			c	d	e	f	g	a	b	cl					
Phrygian				d	e	f	g	a	b	cl	dl				
Dorian					e	f	g	a	b	cl	dl	el			
Hypolydian						f	g	a	b	cl	dl	el	fl		
Hypophrygian							g	a	b	cl	dl	el	fl	gl	
Hypodorian								a	b	cl	dl	el	fl	gl	al

Species of the octave

Note. The Lesser Perfect System consisted of the octave from Proslambanomenos to Mese *plus* the tetrachord Synemmenon (Trite, Paranete, Nete = b♭ cl dl).

The Greater Perfect System and the species of the octave are given here in *diatonic* form only; the "standing-notes", that mark the limit of the tetrachords, are indicated by asterisks. For the effect of chromatic and enharmonic variation upon the forms of the octave-species see pp. 14–16.

I. INDEX OF PROPER NAMES

(The small numbers refer to footnotes. Page references in heavier type refer to the main treatment of a subject.)

II. INDEX OF TERMS

III. INDEX OF PASSAGES